HOW TO
TAKE BACK
OUR GOVERNMENT
— AND —
OUR NATION
— FROM —
CORRUPT POLITICIANS

POLITICIANS' FITNESS FOR PUBLIC OFFICE

LENNOX JOHN GRANT

WESTBOW
PRESS®
A DIVISION OF THOMAS NELSON
& ZONDERVAN

WestBow Press books may be ordered through booksellers or by contacting:

WestBow Press
A Division of Thomas Nelson & Zondervan
1663 Liberty Drive
Bloomington, IN 47403
www.westbowpress.com
1 (866) 928-1240

Scripture quotations marked NKJV are taken from the New King James Version®. Copyright © 1982 by Thomas Nelson. Used by permission. All rights reserved.

Scripture quotations marked ISV are taken from The Holy Bible: International Standard Version. Release 2.0, Build 2015.02.09. Copyright © 1995-2014 by ISV Foundation. ALL RIGHTS RESERVED INTERNATIONALLY. Used by permission of Davidson Press, LLC.

Scripture quotations marked KJV are taken from the King James Version.

ISBN: 978-1-9736-9708-4 (sc)
ISBN: 978-1-9736-9710-7 (hc)
ISBN: 978-1-9736-9709-1 (e)

Library of Congress Control Number: 2020913092

Print information available on the last page.

WestBow Press rev. date: 08/07/2020

All credit, praise, and glory go to the Lord and Savior Jesus Christ for the wisdom contained in this book.

.

To my beloved wife, Shaffina, who has since gone home to be with the Lord, and who made great personal sacrifices to allow me to follow God's calling in my life

CONTENTS

INTRODUCTION

All over the world, people are lamenting corruption in government. These lamentations have manifested themselves in much public outcry and in some instances, violent street protests.

The news clippings below represent a few examples of the reports of the public's outcry against this scourge in many nations.

> A quarter-million Brazilians took to the streets in the latest a wave of sometimes-violent protests that are increasingly focusing on corruption and reforming a government system in which people have lost faith. A new poll shows that 75 percent of citizens support the demonstrations.[1]

> After massive public outcry over revelations of alleged widespread corruption in Trinidad and Tobago's Ministry of Sport's LifeSport programme, Minister of Sport Anil Roberts has resigned from his ministerial post. His resignation letter expressed a "desire" to resign both as minister and as parliamentary representative for the country's D'Abadie/ O'Meara constituency.[2]

> Several of Kenya's top government ministers stepped down Saturday after Kenyan President Uhuru Kenyatta asked high-ranking officials

named in an ongoing corruption probe to leave their offices, according to a report.[3]

Tens of thousands of people have turned out in the streets of Malaysia's capital to demand that Prime Minister Najib Razak step down amid what opponents are calling a massive corruption scandal. The country's former leader, Mahathir Mohamad made a surprise appearance at the anti-government rally in Kuala Lumpur, Reuters reports.[4]

Every Saturday for nearly two months, Constitution Square outside Guatemala City's National Palace has overflowed with thousands of protesters demanding an end to corruption and the resignation of President Otto Perez Molina.

Most are from the young, middle-class, smartphone generation, and they organize the leaderless demonstrations through social media. But there are also priests standing shoulder-to-shoulder with businessmen, and students alongside homemakers, in what Guatemala analysts call an unprecedented mass mobilization cutting across socio-economic, political, even class lines.[5]

As the sky dims over the Honduran capital, the streets are ablaze with the flames of thousands of torches, each one carried by a citizen outraged by the entrenched corruption and impunity in this Central American country. Though the light from the bamboo torches gives the protest a festive air, the message the protesters are sending is serious. One handmade sign reads "The corrupt have ripped apart my country." Another says: "Enough is enough."[6]

Other states have plenty of corruption, but it's hard to beat New York when it comes to sheer volume. The criminal complaint Monday against Dean Skelos, the state Senate majority leader, and his son Adam came just three months after charges were brought against Sheldon Silver, then the Assembly Speaker. Having the top leaders in both chambers face criminal charges in the same session is an unparalleled achievement, but Skelos is now the fifth straight Senate majority leader in Albany to face them.[7]

Canada's main opposition party has called for federal police to probe whether members of the prime minister's office were involved in a bribery and expenses affair that has engulfed the ruling Conservatives.[8]

Corruption in nearly half the world's nations is not getting much better and, indeed, in many countries is intensifying—affecting virtually every aspect of life among peoples on every continent.

While a year ago, some 72 out of 158 nations surveyed by the international watchdog group

Transparency International were classified as "corrupt," now 74 of 163 countries fall into the same category. A few, most notably India, managed to bootstrap themselves (just barely) out of the truly corrupt group, while others, particularly Iran, dug themselves more firmly into that camp.[9]

What common mistake are we, as electors, making in the choice of candidates who cause us to elect corrupt individuals to public office? Such public outcry is not new. It has occurred time and time again throughout history as nations and civilizations descended into moral, spiritual, and social decadence.

The Bible is replete with records of such public outcries by the prophets of the nation of Israel as they acted as the voice of the conscience of God and sought to bring the people unto repentance.

One such instance of public lamentation is by the prophet Isaiah in the book of Isaiah:

> How the faithful city has become a harlot! It was full of justice; Righteousness lodged in it, But now murderers. Your silver has become dross, Your wine mixed with water. Your princes are rebellious, And companions of thieves; Everyone loves bribes, And follows after rewards. They do not defend the fatherless, Nor does the cause of the widow come before them. (Isaiah 1:21–23 NKJV)

Isaiah began by describing the former state of the city and went on to describe the decadence into which the city had fallen. First, he laments "how the faithful city has become a harlot" (Isaiah 1:21 NKJV).

How could a city that once derived its wide renown, blessings, and miraculous military victories through its worship of the true and living God for several centuries have turned away from that God and turned to serving idols and images of stone of wood and silver?

Secondly, Isaiah says the city "was full of justice" (Isaiah 1:21 NKJV). The city's judiciary once executed justice for the people; they maintained the cause of the oppressed, punished the wicked, and vindicated those whose rights were violated. Everyone had the "right to an effective remedy and to a fair trial,"[10] and the poor, the widowed, and the fatherless were adequately cared for.

Thirdly "righteousness lodged in it" (Isaiah 1:21 NKJV). That meant that the blessings of God were on the people, which resulted in prosperity and right living. Moral and spiritual values were adhered to, and crimes were near absent.

Having reminisced on the city's former state, Isaiah turned to mourn the corruption into which it had fallen. The city was overrun with criminal activity, "but now murders" (Isaiah 1:21 NKJV).

Most shocking of all, evil and wickedness had taken control of the corridors of power and the halls of justice. The rulers of all persons had now forsaken the law of God: "Your princes are rebellious" (Isaiah 1:23 NKJV).

The rulers who had sworn "to uphold the constitution and the law" and "to do right to all manner of people without fear or favor, affection, or ill will"[11] had become "companion of thieves" (Isaiah 1:23 NKJV).

Bribery had become institutionalized, and the rulers were accepting bribes and demanding kickbacks. "Everyone loves bribes, and follows after rewards" (Isaiah 1:23 NKJV).

In other words, the foundations were being destroyed or had already collapsed. The moral, social, and spiritual institutions that were established to preserve the nation's peace and prosperity had collapsed, and the prophet, as God's conscience, lamented the latter state of the nation.

Isaiah's description of Israel back then can be applied to the corruption that exists in many nations of the world today. There is no respect for the rule of law, and there is widespread embezzlement, waste, incompetence, mismanagement, and nepotism.

Israel was a theocracy that later became a monarchy. In either case, the rulers were appointed for life. There were no elections, which meant they could not remove rebellious and corrupt leaders and replace them with a new government. When wickedness and corruption crept into the government, they were stuck with it for a lifetime in most instances.

Today, many countries have a system that gives us the constitutional right to replace a corrupt and wicked government and elect men and women who we believe will execute justice and preserve the moral, social, and spiritual institutions that establish the state.

However, we have serious challenges in effectively separating the sheep from the goats when we are asked to elect candidates to public office.

CHAPTER 1

THE CHALLENGE FACING THE ELECTORATE

Every two, four, or five years, depending on which country or state they live in, citizens are called upon to elect officials to public office to look after their people's business. These are the men and women we entrust with the public purse, the governance of the affairs, and the business of state.

Most of the time, this call to elect public officials is a very challenging exercise for the electorate. We must decipher the crafty public relations glitz and platform utterances disseminated by candidates regarding their lofty promises, sometimes exaggerated experiences, qualifications, and competencies. We also must battle with our own racial, ethnic, educational, and social biases in making judgments about who is fit for public office.

Because we, as citizens, lack simple, clear, and consistent criteria by which to assess the suitability of candidates who offer themselves for public office, we are often deceived by political rhetoric into making the wrong choices and electing political misfits. We end up paying a heavy price for doing so in the form of atrocious governance. Many times, the officials we elect turn out to be incompetent and/or corrupt. They serve the interests of their financiers, their friends, and their families. This is a major problem for which we, the citizenry, need to find a solution.

What criteria can we use to more objectively determine if a person is fit for public office, is the best candidate for an office, or is fit to be entrusted with the authority to control the affairs and business of the state? Having failed in our efforts at establishing simple, clear, consistent, and effective benchmarks that laymen can understand, it may be worthwhile to consider what the omniscient God, the ancient of days, has to say on this matter.

CHAPTER 2

GOD'S CRITERIA FOR SELECTING PERSONS FIT FOR PUBLIC OFFICE

Moreover you shall select from all the people able men, as fear God, men of truth, hating covetousness. And place such over them to be rulers of thousands, and rulers of hundreds, rulers of fifties, and rulers of tens. And let them judge the people at all times.

—Exodus 18:21–22 (NKJV)

This was the advice Jethro—a priest of God and Moses's father-in-law—gave to Moses when he needed to put some governance structures in place to effectively rule the Israelites during their sojourn in the wilderness.

The criteria are very few in number, very clear, very simple, and very effective when closely examined and considered. To reiterate Jethro's recommendations, he said that those who were to be selected to govern the people were to be:

- able men
- men who fear God
- men of truth
- men who hate covetousness

Let's examine these criteria more closely, one at a time, in the following chapters.

CHAPTER 3

THEY MUST BE ABLE AND COMPETENT

They must be able, qualified, and competent. This seems pretty straightforward. We all know and expect those elected to public office should be qualified and competent to do their job. However, the Hebrew word that is translated as "able" in English is the word "Khah'-yil" (phonetic spelling)[12] which connotes strength, virtue, and valor.

Hence, the person identified as a candidate for public office, in addition to being academically qualified, must also be a person of strength and valor. They should be courageous and strong. They should be fearless in the face of difficulty, criticism, or danger. And they should be fearless in the pursuit of justice. They should not be a coward or afraid to stand for justice or what is right. They should defend the rights of the people. Mere academic qualifications are not enough. A man or woman could be highly qualified—and still be a wimp who could easily be influenced or manipulated by the rich and powerful or the enemies of the people.

For public office, academic qualifications and the ability to carry out professional duties do not necessarily equal competence. This raises the question of whether we are training our young men and women to be truly competent.

Many times, because of a lack of wisdom, we do not scrutinize our choice of political candidates for Khah'-yil[13] (strength, virtue, and valor). Many times, also for reasons of political patronage, incompetent individuals are appointed to offices of public trust with disastrous consequences. We all have expressed our own frustrations as part of the litany of lamentations provoked by the disastrous societal fallout due to incompetence in public office.

CHAPTER 4

THEY MUST BE PERSONS WHO FEAR GOD

The fear of the Lord is the beginning of knowledge: but fools despise wisdom and instruction.
—Proverbs 1:7 (NKJV)

The fear of the Lord is the beginning of wisdom: and the knowledge of the holy is understanding.
—Proverbs 9:10 (KJV)

"The fear of the Lord" (Proverbs 1:7 KJV) does not mean to be afraid of the Lord as though He is a terrible judge who is waiting to pounce on you to punish or crush you at the slightest mistake. The scriptures teach that God is love. There could not be anyone more loving than the Lord. The scripture portrays Him as the Good Shepherd and loving Savior:

> The Lord is merciful and gracious, slow to anger, and plenteous in mercy. He will not always chide: neither will he keep his anger forever. (Psalm 103:8–9 KJV)

The fear of the Lord in the context of the two scriptures above means to acknowledge that:

- He is the true and living God.
- He is wiser than us all.
- He is omniscient.
- God is the counselor of all counselors in all matters that pertain to life, godliness, and integrity.
- God does care and takes pleasure in intervening in the affairs of humans for the good of His creation.
- God is to be respected, esteemed, and revered for His great love toward us, His omnipotence, and His omniscience.

Christ is called the "wonderful counsellor" (Isaiah 9:6 KJV)

- He is the Senior Counsel (SC) of All Senior Counsels.
- He is the Queen's Counsel of All Queen's Counsels.
- He is the first to be awarded silk. As a matter of fact, He is the author of silk.

The person who fears God submits to the counsel of God. They acknowledge God as their senior counsel and his personal advisor.

God says in His Word, "You shall not steal" (Exodus 20:15 NKJV). The person who fears God will obey that admonition. All public officials need advisors. In very important matters, even attorneys retain senior counsel. Public officials also need senior counsel in important matters pertaining to affairs of the state, life, godliness, and honesty.

Only a fool or an idiot would appoint a person to manage their affairs who refuses to listen to—or does not acknowledge—the advice of senior counsel.

Those who fear God seek wisdom and understanding from the Senior Counsel of All Senior Counsels.

If any of you lacks wisdom, let him ask of God, who gives to all liberally and without reproach, and it will be given to him. (James 1:5 NKJV)

At Gibeon the Lord appeared to Solomon in a dream by night; and God said, "Ask! What shall I give you?" And Solomon said: "You have shown great mercy to Your servant David my father, because he walked before You in truth, in righteousness, and in uprightness of heart with You; You have continued this great kindness for him, and You have given him a son to sit on his throne, as it is this day. Now, O Lord my God, You have made Your servant king instead of my father David, but I am a little child; I do not know how to go out or come in. And Your servant is in the midst of Your people whom You have chosen, a great people, too numerous to be numbered or counted. Therefore give to Your servant an understanding heart to judge Your people, that I may discern between good and evil. For who is able to judge this great people of Yours?" The speech pleased the Lord, that Solomon had asked this thing. Then God said to him: "Because you have asked this thing, and have not asked long life for yourself, nor have asked riches for yourself, nor have asked the life of your enemies, but have asked for yourself understanding to discern justice, behold, I have done according to your words; see, I have given you a wise and understanding heart, so that there has not been anyone like you before you, nor shall any like you arise after you. And I have also given you what you have not asked: both riches and honor, so that there shall not be anyone like you among the kings all your days." (1 Kings 3:5–13 NKJV)

Those who do not fear God either reject or ignore the advice of the Senior Counsel of All Senior Counsels.

The public official who ignores the advice of the Senior Counsel of All Senior Counsels is a grave liability to the state and the party that they represent.

The problems with many people who are elected to public office are at least fourfold:

- On the one hand, they may be unaware that they can ask God for wisdom to govern.
- On the other hand, they may feel that they are not worthy enough to approach God to ask for anything.
- They are filled with pride. They are averse to the idea of humbling themselves before the Almighty God, their Creator. They refuse to acknowledge their own ignorance and inadequacies to manage the complexities of life and the affairs of the state. They do not ask for wisdom. They perceive this as weakness.
- Many are outright corrupt, and they despise God's counsel. They think their reputations, support from their network of peers, and research data are the only things needed for the task at hand. They think educational, academic, and professional achievements and competencies—coupled with attendance at management conferences and workshops—are all that are required. That is why we have been unable to resolve difficult national and global issues.

CHAPTER 5

THE SHORT PRAYER THAT MADE A YOUNG KING THE WISEST RULER OF ALL TIME

Suddenly thrust into the office of the king, an unprepared and naïve young man became the wisest and greatest ruler who ever lived because he was humble enough to ask wisdom to govern.

The account of King Solomon's ascendancy to the throne can be found in (1 Kings 3:5-13)

When Solomon ascended the throne of his father, King David, he was young and naive. Acknowledging his ignorance and inability to govern the great nation of Israel, and in response to God's invitation for him to ask for what he wants, He said to God:

> Give your servant an understanding mind to govern your people, so I can discern between good and evil. Otherwise, how will I be able to govern this great people of yours? (1 Kings 3:9 ISV)

God's answer to Solomon is very interesting:

> And the speech pleased the Lord, that Solomon had asked this thing. And God said unto him, Because thou hast asked this thing, and hast not asked for thyself long life; neither hast asked riches for thyself, nor hast asked the life

of thine enemies; but hast asked for thyself understanding to discern judgment; Behold, I have done according to thy words: lo, I have given thee a wise and an understanding heart; so that there was none like thee before thee, neither after thee shall any arise like unto thee. And I have also given thee that which thou hast not asked, both riches, and honor: so that there shall not be any among the kings like unto thee all thy days. (1 Kings 3:10–13 KJV)

And God gave Solomon wisdom and understanding exceeding much, and largeness of heart, even as the sand that is on the sea shore. And Solomon's wisdom excelled the wisdom of all the children of the east country, and all the wisdom of Egypt. (1 Kings 4:29–30 KJV)

The rest is history. Under King Solomon, Israel's greatness as a nation was exceedingly enhanced. Solomon became so wise that it is recorded of him:

And there came of all people to hear the Wisdom of Solomon, from all kings of the earth, which had heard of his wisdom. (1 Kings 4:34 KJV)

So King Solomon exceeded all the kings of the earth for riches and for wisdom. And all the earth sought to Solomon, to hear his wisdom, which God had put in his heart. And they brought every man his present, vessels of silver, and vessels of gold, and garments, and armour,

and spices, horses, and mules, a rate year by year.
(1 Kings 10:23–25 KJV)

Notice that the wisdom Solomon received from God brought him great favor with all the kings of the earth, and they enriched him further with their presents of precious commodities.

The queen of Sheba visited Solomon to confirm the reports of his wisdom and riches. She was completely overwhelmed by what she heard and saw:

> It was a true report that I heard in mine own land of thy acts and of thy wisdom. Howbeit I believed not the words, until I came, and mine eyes had seen it: and, behold, the half was not told me: thy wisdom and prosperity exceedeth the fame which I heard. (1 Kings 10:6–7 KJV)

> Blessed be the Lord thy God, which delighted in thee, to set thee on the throne of Israel: because the Lord loved Israel for ever, therefore made he thee king, to do judgment and justice. (1 Kings 10:9 KJV)

> And she gave the king an hundred and twenty talents of gold, and of spices very great store, and precious stones: there came no more such abundance of spices as these which the queen of Sheba gave to King Solomon.[1] (1 Kings 10:10 KJV)

---

[1] 120 talents of gold is approximately equal to 131,946 troy ounces. At today's price of US $1,572 per ounce, 120 talents of gold is worth $207.4 million.

So much for the results of a prayer that lasted for just fifteen seconds! Imagine that! God always graciously rewards those who seek to execute His justice in the earth. God is not looking for lengthy oratory when we approach his throne.

Daniel was a high-ranking public official in the kingdom of Babylon, yet he found time to pray and give God thanks three times a day:

> Now when Daniel knew that the writing was signed, he went home. And in his upper room, with his windows open toward Jerusalem, he knelt down on his knees three times that day, and prayed and gave thanks before his God, as was his custom since early days. (Daniel 6:10 NKJV)

Solomon's request was remarkable:

- It was a very short and simple prayer (just about fifteen seconds).
- Solomon referred to himself as God's servant. He understood he was a steward and not a lord over the people.
- God answered his prayer immediately—as soon as he finished the last syllable of his speech.

Too many public officials are unaware of the fact that they are accountable to God for the people they govern. As a ruler or public official, you must realize that you are first God's servant. The people you govern are God's creations.

> God stands in the congregation of the mighty;
> He judges among the gods. How long will you

judge unjustly, And show partiality to the wicked? Selah Defend the poor and fatherless; Do justice to the afflicted and needy. Deliver the poor and needy; Free them from the hand of the wicked. (Psalm 82:1-4 NKJV)

And God said to Solomon, "Because this was in thine heart, and thou hast not asked riches, wealth, or honor, nor the life of thine enemies, neither yet hast asked for long life, but hast asked wisdom and knowledge for thyself, that thou mayest judge My people over whom I have made thee king, wisdom and knowledge is granted unto thee; and I will give thee riches and wealth and honor, such as none of the kings have had who have been before thee, neither shall there any after thee have the like. (2 Chronicles 1:11–12 NKJV)

Why did God ask King Solomon the question in the first place? The scripture we just read is very revealing. God was testing Solomon to see if he was a typical politician or public official in high office whose primary motives for seeking public office were to:

- Enrich themselves (get riches and wealth). High public office gives either direct or indirect access to the public purse.
- Obtain honor (high esteem in the sight of men; to enjoy the privileges and prerogatives that come with high office).
- Use political power to eliminate or neutralize their enemies and political opponents.

- Use political power to extend their time in public office.

However, this scripture reveals to us that God would exalt that public official whose primary motive for seeking public office is to execute justice for the people. God would give them riches, wealth, and honor.

It is also worth noting that the elected public official with selfish motives cannot count on receiving God's wisdom to make them a wise leader or count on receiving wealth from God. It should be very clear to the reader by now that the Lord will bless and give divine wisdom to those who are humble!

> God resisteth the proud, and giveth grace to the humble. (1 Peter 5:5 KJV)

The meaning of the word *proud* in this passage is not as much about having a high opinion of yourself in relation to others as it is about having an opinion of yourself in which you believe that you are self-sufficient and don't need God's counsel. You believe that you can get by on your own intelligence and strength.

God is saying such individuals cannot expect to receive anything from Him. He will be reluctant to release His grace, divine wisdom, and power to work through such a one when you are faced with difficulties. This lack of humility is responsible for many of the troubles that individuals and societies face. These people do not submit to the counsel of God!

God will do great wonders with anyone who humbles themselves before Him. Those who acknowledge their own limitations, weaknesses, and incapacities can depend upon God. God's grace—His mighty, wonder-working miracle power—is available to work in, through, and on behalf of any such person. What a blessing this is!

The wisdom of Christ is available to kings, rulers, princes, judges, and nobles who desire, like King Solomon, to have "an understanding mind to govern" (1 Kings 3:9 ISV) their people justly so they "can discern between good and evil" (1 Kings 3:9 ISV).

> Counsel is mine and sound wisdom; I am understanding, I have strength. By me Kings reign, and princes decree justice. By me princes rule and nobles, even all the judges of the earth. I love them that love me, and those that seek me early shall find me. (Proverbs 8:14–17 NKJV)

CHAPTER 6

THEY MUST HATE COVETOUSNESS

Covetous is synonymous with the words cupidity, greed, rapacious, and avaricious. *Miriam Webster's Dictionary of Synonyms* defines these terms as follows:

> Cupidity, greed, rapacity, and avarice are comparable when meaning intense desire for wealth or possessions.

> Covetous is having or manifesting a strong desire for possessions, especially material possessions. Covetous implies inordinateness of desire.

> Cupidity stresses the intensity and compelling nature of the desire and often suggests covetousness as well.

> Greed, more than cupidity, implies a controlling passion. It suggests not strong, but inordinate desire, and it commonly connotes meanness as well.

> Rapacity implies both cupidity and the actual seizing or snatching of what one especially desires—and anything else that will satisfy one's

greed of money and property. It often suggests extortion, plunder, or oppressive exactions.

Avarice involves the idea of cupidity—and often carries a strong suggestion of rapacity—but it stresses miserliness and implies an unwillingness to let go of whatever wealth or property one has acquired and an insatiable greed for more.

In summary, it can be said that a covetous person has an inordinate, insatiable, uncontrollable, passionate desire for accumulating or hoarding wealth, money, and property and will engage in extortion, plunder, and—if need be—oppressive exactions to acquire them.

As public officials, they will unashamedly rape the government or state treasury, extort, plunder, and exact state assets to enrich themselves, their friends, their financiers, and their families. They engage in elaborate schemes that are designed to exchange political favors for financial kickbacks in a variety of ways, including money in foreign bank accounts, state contracts, insider trading, and exorbitant campaign donations.

This criterion is especially important when the elected public official will be working in an environment where the checks and balances are weak and/or ineffective. If there are loopholes to escape justice, they will have to regulate their own behaviors:

And you shall take no bribe, for a bribe blinds the discerning and perverts the words of the righteous. (Exodus 23:8 NKJV)

You shall not pervert justice; you shall not show partiality, nor take a bribe, for a bribe blinds

the eyes of the wise and twists the words of the
righteous. (Deuteronomy 16:19 NKJV)

These scriptures clearly reveal that taking bribes is a very
destructive practice. They clearly reveal that when a wise
man takes a bribe, he becomes "blind." They lose the ability
to process *light*—wisdom and truth—even when that wisdom
and truth are streaming toward them. They lose the ability to
discern right from wrong, good from evil, and truth from error.
Under such circumstances, they become practitioners of deceit!

Public officials who take bribes lose their vision and are no
longer able to make wise and just decisions in the best interests of
all the people. The scripture says they are blind! God the Creator
says they are blind! This blindness is of such a pernicious nature
that they are unable to discern what is in the best interests of the
people—and they are unable to discern even what is inimical to
their own corrupt racket. In other words, they will continue with
their fiendish zeal to embark on courses of action that expose
their iniquity to all and lead to their eventual downfall.

Those who take bribes are breaking a spiritual law, and the
consequence of that is "blindness." What is remarkable about
these scriptures is that they both state that a bribe blinds the
eyes of the wise. It does not blind the stupid, those of mediocre
intelligence, the ignorant, or the uneducated; it blinds the wise.
Imagine that! How pathetic!

When the quoted scriptures were written, blindness was
considered a pitiable disability. In those days, the blind were
rendered poor, incapacitated, and helpless. In fact, many of
them ended up being beggars and were not able to make any
meaningful contributions to society. The moral of the proverb
is that those who are blind are unfit to govern!

Hans Christian Andersen wrote a famous story entitled "The Emperor's New Clothes"

> I can now understand why the great emperor in the story was so blind. He could not see the so-called new clothes the rogues had made for him. Most likely, he was a corrupt man who was taking bribes. He must have been playing smart with crookedness! His blindness permeated the whole society to such an extent that it had to take the truly innocent, a child, to point out the emperor's folly.

The consequences of this diabolical practice are so destructive that God instructs the wise ruler to promptly excise from his cabinet any officer who is guilty of such conduct:

> A wicked man accepts a bribe behind the back to pervert the ways of justice. (Proverbs 17:23 NKJV)

> A wise king sifts out the wicked, and brings the threshing wheel over them. (Proverbs 20:26 NKJV)

> Take away the wicked from before the king, and his throne shall be established in righteousness. (Proverbs 25:5 KJV)

We readily acknowledge the consequences associated with the violation of natural laws, and we are very aware of the consequence of violating the law of gravity. You know with certainty what to expect if you jump off the protective railing of a fifteenth-floor hotel room.

Except for the spiritually discerning, most people—even well-educated people— are ignorant of the existence of spiritual laws and their consequences. There are spiritual laws, and there are real consequences for breaking them.

The ruler who takes bribes destroys his nation:

> The king establishes the land by justice, but he who receives bribes overthrows it. (Proverbs 29:4 NKJV)

This scripture is especially remarkable in revealing that the ruler or public official who takes bribes overthrows his country. The word *overthrow* is synonymous with the words *ruin, subvert, bankrupt, wreck,* and *destroy.* The ruler who takes bribes will overthrow, subvert, bankrupt, wreck, and destroy their country. They will be responsible for the creation of a failed state.

Of course, this is not surprising and is to be expected. We have already seen that those who take bribes are unfit to govern.

Two thousand years ago, Jesus Christ warned the people of His day of what to expect of leaders who become blind:

> Let them alone: they be blind leaders of the blind. And if the blind lead the blind, both shall fall into the ditch. (Matthew 15:14 KJV)

Another evil that is associated with the one taking bribes is the blight of deceit:

- a bribe perverts the words of the righteous (Exodus 23:8; NKJV)
- a bribe twists the words of the righteous (Deuteronomy 16:19 NKJV)

Noah Webster's 1828 *Dictionary of American English* defines *to pervert*:

> 1. To turn from truth, propriety, or from its proper purpose; to distort from its true use or end; as, to pervert reason by misdirecting it; to pervert the laws by misinterpreting and misapplying them; to pervert justice; to pervert the meaning of an author; to pervert nature; to pervert truth.
>
> 2. To turn from the right; to corrupt.

In other words, the person who takes bribes is corrupt and soon becomes a practitioner of deceit.

What is remarkable here about these scriptures is that they both teach that a bribe corrupts the words of the righteous. It is not the sinner or the vile and debased person; it is the righteous! How shocking! Can you imagine that!

Many of us have been very perplexed, bewildered, puzzled, and troubled by the pronouncements and remarks of religious leaders—ministers of the Gospel who are esteemed by many—but who for some inexplicable reasons on occasions "call evil good, and good evil" (Isaiah 5:20 KJV). They seem to justify the wicked and condemn the just.

Our Father is omniscient and cannot lie. He has given us the answer to this enigma by revelation through the scriptures quoted above. The answer? The righteous ones pervert their words when they are receiving gifts (bribes).

Another despicable practice we observe in our society is white-collar criminals being extolled by their friends and supporters. There was a time not too long ago when the princes in our society were exemplars and excellent role models who spoke out against corruption and immorality and executed justice for the people. Many of those in high office and in esteemed professions have now forsaken God's law; they are now companions of thieves!

They are the ones who—though being aware of the wicked deeds and clandestine criminal activities of their associates and the havoc they wreak on our nations, especially our young people—hide behind their professional titles and respectable facades and abuse their seemingly good standing in society by stoutly defending and extolling the "morality" and "integrity" of those who are blatantly corrupt. We are now at a point where many within the circle of these criminals respect them for their cunning and their ability to abuse their ingenuity to frustrate the arms of justice. The Word of God is a "discerner of the thoughts and intents of the heart." (Hebrews 4:12 NKJV):

> They that forsake the law praise the wicked.
> (Proverbs 28:4 KJV)

It is those who are backslidden in their hearts and whose consciences have been desensitized by their continuous racket that do such things. They are playing smart with crookedness!

They are the same ones who connive to rape the public purse of billions of dollars while accusing workers who seek just increases in wages of being greedy and endangering economic development. Rightly did Isaiah the prophet speak of them when he said:

> Thy princes are rebellious, and companions of thieves: every one loveth gifts, and followeth after rewards: they judge not the fatherless, neither doth the cause of the widow come unto them. (Isaiah 1:23 KJV)

They love bribes, and they run after kickbacks! They really do not care about the people! They deceive themselves into thinking that we are all a bunch of morons whose only noble aspiration, like chimpanzees in a cage, is to full our bellies.

That is the kind of indignity with which they look upon the people whom they purport to represent. They seem to be totally unaware of the righteous indignation their racket has provoked in the spirits of the majority of ordinary, decent, law-abiding citizens. This is why, today, around the world, people are taking to the streets in the tens of thousands to protest against these criminals and their nefarious deeds. People are saying, "Enough is enough!" They are infuriated and fed up! They are clamoring for good governance!

> He that saith unto the wicked, Thou art righteous; him shall the people curse, nations shall abhor him. (Proverbs 24:24 KJV)

CHAPTER 7

THE MISSION OF THE KING

The king establishes the land by justice, but he
who receives bribes overthrows it.
—Proverbs 29:4 (NKJV)

The mission of the office of the king, the prime minister, or the executive president of a nation is the execution of justice. The ruler is God's servant executing Justice for the people.

A ruler executes justice by influencing and acting as a compelling advocate for the implementation of policies and programs and the enactment of laws that liberate the people and set them free from all oppression.

They should be liberators and not oppressors. As liberators, they lead the fight against corruption in government and in the affairs of the state. Together with the ministers of government, they harness all the weapons in the state's legal, financial, economic, and law enforcement arsenals to repress corruption and liberate the oppressed.

> They that forsake the law praise the wicked:
> but such as keep the law contend with them.
> (Proverbs 28:4 KJV)

God views such a ruler as cooperating with Him in executing His will on the earth and is therefore worthy of special honor and rewards:

He who says to the wicked, "You are righteous,"
Him the people will curse; Nations will abhor
him. But those who rebuke the wicked will have
delight, And a good blessing will come upon
them. (Proverbs 24:24–25 NKJV)

Yes, God will reward those rulers who use the authority
delegated to them to stamp out corruption in government and
the affairs of the state—with delight and good blessings. A just
ruler facilitates the enforcement of laws that disarm oppressors.
They do not facilitate the escape of oppressors from facing
justice for their misdeeds. Liberators concern themselves with
how the state can utilize its resources to:

- develop the nation's human capital
- bring relief to the poor, the needy, the destitute, and the
  socially displaced
- ease the burdens of the elderly
- assist the differently abled in fulfilling their potential
- assist the less fortunate in getting an education
- assist the less fortunate in getting the health care they need
- create employment for the unemployed
- ensure that all have equal access to public goods and
  services
- further economic and social development

They address the needs of the 99 percent working and middle
classes while not totally ignoring the wants of the super wealthy
1 percent. The mission of the office of the king, the prime
minister, or the executive president of a nation is the execution
of justice:

Rulers who execute justice for their people bring stability

to their nations. Justice establishes the nation, and it makes the nation resistant to moral, social, and economic decay and disintegration. Corruption and bribery destabilize the moral, social, and economic fabric of a nation.

King David understood quite clearly the need for nations to be governed by just rulers and the benefits that accrue to a nation that is governed by such people. When he was old and about to die, these were his last words to his son Solomon who was about to ascend the throne:

> The Spirit of the Lord spoke by me, And His word was on my tongue. The God of Israel said, The Rock of Israel spoke to me: "He who rules over men must be just, Ruling in the fear of God. And he shall be like the light of the morning when the sun rises, A morning without clouds, Like the tender grass springing out of the earth, By clear shining after rain." (2 Samuel 23:2–4 NKJV)

This scripture echoes the truth expounded earlier in this chapter that rulers and public officials are called to execute justice for their people. They must be just!

> He that ruleth over men must be just. (2 Samuel 23:3 KJV)

The scripture also reinforces what was explained in chapter 4 that those identified as candidates for public office must fear God.

As was explained in chapter 4, the person who fears God acknowledges God's omniscience and omnipotence and submits to God's will and counsel in matters of life and as it relates to godliness and integrity in the affairs of the state.

This scripture also alludes to—and gives beautiful and profound insights to—the blessings that accrue to a nation or people governed by officials who are just and who rule in the fear of God. It describes rulers and public officials who are just and rule in the fear of God:

> The light of the morning, when the sun rises; a morning without clouds. (2 Samuel 23:4 NKJV)

The most salient phenomenon about the rising of the sun is that it dispels the darkness. Likewise, the election of just rulers who fear God to positions of leadership and public office signal the dispelling of the darkness of corruption in government and all that goes with it.

When electrical power returns after an outage and the lights are turned on again, you can hear the relieved voices of everyone in your home or office or at the neighbors next door. When the light appears again, there is rejoicing and cheering. Everybody exhales and says, "Ah! Thank God the lights have returned!"

Even so, when just rulers are promoted to leadership in a nation or state, the scripture says:

> When the righteous are in authority, the people rejoice: but when the wicked beareth rule, the people mourn. (Proverbs 29:2 KJV)

> When it goeth well with the righteous, the city rejoiceth: and when the wicked perish, there is shouting. (Proverbs 11:10 KJV)

> The light of the morning when the sun rises; a
> morning without clouds. (2 Samuel 23:4 NKJV)

This beautiful metaphor suggests the dawning of a new day, a fresh start without daunting difficulties and/or uncertainties

As the day dawns and the sun rises on a cloudless morning, the engines of economic activity are restarted. There is renewed confidence, enthusiasm, joy, and excitement to do new things, pursue new goals, and contribute to the development of the social and economic well-being of the village, the community, the city, the town, and the nation.

Confidence is renewed, enthusiasm is renewed, and expectations are revived. Dismay and uncertainties diminish because the people do not perceive the dark clouds of corrupt governance—waste, mismanagement, and nepotism—that can turn all their hard work and effort into futility.

The farmers and shepherds briskly take their flocks out to graze, and the shopkeepers lustily swing open their doors. There is renewed confidence and expectation that things will get done, goals will be accomplished, and aspirations will be achieved:

Such is the impact that kings, prime ministers, presidents, and senior public officials who are just and who rule in the fear of God have on the people they govern. They inspire hope, confidence, enthusiasm, and a willingness to achieve in the people they govern.

These are the representatives of the people who take their oath of office seriously: "to bear true faith and allegiance" to their nations, to "uphold the Constitution and the law," to "conscientiously and impartially and to the best" of their ability discharge their duties to the people of their nation "and to do right to all manner of people without fear or favor, affection or ill-will." [14]

Conversely, those who govern by unjust decrees and corrupt practices provoke vexation, anxiety, and uncertainty among the people. Their modus operandi—being founded on bribery, nepotism, and corruption—creates moral, social, and economic instability that invokes lamentations of deep grief among the people. They are like dark, ominous clouds in the monsoon or rainy season that come in from afar, dumping their heavy cargo on the earth, flooding the cities, and creating havoc and consternation in every place. When they move on, they leave a trail of destruction and ruin that has to be cleaned up by those who come after.

Corrupt governance further exacerbates instability by triggering frequent changes of government.

> For the transgression of a land many are the princes thereof: but by a man of understanding and knowledge the state thereof shall be prolonged. (Proverbs 28:2 KJV)

Before the new government can settle in properly and fully develop and execute whatever good policies and programs it may have, it has to hastily exit office. Its corrupt practices and incompetence provoke public outcries, protests, civil disobedience, and calls for the ruler and their government to go!

If the incoming government is itself no better, its time in office will also be troubled and limited to one term. It will not have any foundation to build on because of the poor performance of the previous government, and it will not be allowed sufficient time to execute whatever good policies and programs it may have.

Corrupt governance does not occur in a vacuum; it starts somewhere. Corrupt governance starts with corrupt officials, and corrupt officials start with individual young men and women whose lives have not been sufficiently affected by moral and spiritual values. In many instances, the society in which they grew up has cast off the restraint of godly fear and has permitted corrupt practices to go unchecked and unpunished.

However, the scripture teaches that this instability in governance that damages and retards the growth, development, and prosperity of a nation can be remedied by the election to office of just leaders—those with understanding and knowledge—who rule in the fear of God.

Jesus told his disciples:

> Ye are the salt of the earth: but if the salt have lost his savour, wherewith shall it be salted? it is thenceforth good for nothing, but to be cast out, and to be trodden under foot of men. (Matthew 5:13 KJV)

The presence in our governments of public officials who can be described as the salt of the earth would greatly retard and sanitize the putrefaction taking place in the affairs of the state.

CHAPTER 8

IDENTIFYING TYRANTS, DESPOTS, AND GREAT OPPRESSORS

> A ruler who lacks understanding is a great oppressor, but he who hates covetousness will prolong his days.
>
> **—Proverbs 28:16 (NKJV)**

This scripture clearly reveals that the ruler who is covetous lacks understanding and is a great oppressor. God says that he is "a great oppressor." This is remarkably frightening. The image of a ruler being an oppressor is already a very troubling one—much more that of a great oppressor. God says he is not only an oppressor but a great oppressor:

> Oppress, v. To burden with cruel or unjust impositions or restraints; subject to a burdensome or harsh exercise of authority or power. (Dictionary.com)

> Oppressor, n. One that oppresses; one that imposes unjust burdens on others; one that harasses others with unjust laws or unreasonable severity. (Noah Webster's 1828 Dictionary of American English)

The word oppressor is synonymous with the words *tyrant; despot, dictator, persecutor,* and *overlord.* (Dictionary.com)

According to Noah Webster's 1828 Dictionary of American English, the word "great" means:

> Large in number; as a great many; a great multitude. Expressing a large, extensive or unusual degree of anything; as great fear; great love; great strength; great wealth; great power; great influence; great folly.

In other words, the scripture implies that the covetous ruler is like a thousand and more tyrants, despots, or dictators put together. This is indeed very frightening, and we should beware of such individuals

Our Father, God, is giving us an insight into the degree of mischief and injustice such an official will inflict upon the people over whom they have control. This is very, very, very frightening. Such a ruler may not appear so in public, but God says he or she is a great tyrant, a great despot, a great dictator, a great oppressor, and a great persecutor. When we encounter such rulers, we are to exercise great spiritual vigilance.

This scripture also reveals that you cannot expect a ruler who is covetous to understand and execute justice. The two characteristics are mutually exclusive. They cannot coexist! Such rulers cause vexation of spirit among the people and inflict great grief, sorrow, hardship, suffering, trouble, misery, and pain on their people.

Let us not lose sight of the fact that many rulers do not exercise executive power of their own free will.

Politics have always been a vocation in which many leaders do the bidding of unseen hands that possess great wealth,

These unseen hands wield powerful and sometimes diabolical influences over high ranking office holders, These unseen hands are the greater tyrants.

> As a roaring lion, and a raging bear; so is a wicked ruler over the poor people. (Proverbs 28:15 KJV)

However, God will shorten the ruler's stay in public office because of their oppression of the people.

> But he who hates covetousness will prolong his days. (Proverbs 28:16 NKJV)

This scripture reveals that the ruler who hates covetousness will have a prolonged stay in public office, and it implies that the covetous ruler's stay in office will be cut short.

> Rob not the poor, because he is poor: neither oppress the afflicted in the gate: For the Lord will plead their cause, and spoil the soul of those that spoiled them. (Proverbs 22:22–23 KJV)

> For the oppression of the poor, for the sighing of the needy, now will I arise, saith the Lord; I will set him in safety from him that puffeth at him. (Psalm 12:5 KJV)

The oppressive practices of tyrants and despots include:

- enacting laws to muzzle the press/media and suppress freedom of speech

- frustrating and blocking the enactment of laws supporting the freedom of information.
- punishing or muzzling whistleblowers
- diluting or repealing laws that protect whistleblowers
- censuring those who expose their wicked deeds by speaking the truth
- tampering with the Constitution through the introduction of bills designed to give them unfair electoral advantages
- creating loopholes in the law by tampering with sections of the law to enable them and/or their supporters and financiers to escape justice
- sacking those of integrity who blow the whistle on corrupt colleagues

If left in office long enough, they become fascists in the ways they govern. The biggest source of wealth in most countries is the public purse. In order to accumulate vast amounts of wealth, the despot needs to control the public purse or the channels flowing from the public purse for as long as possible. To do so, they and their cronies have to remain in power for as long as possible. To remain in power for as long as possible, they have to become fascists. (Appendix D contains a more detailed description of the practices of oppressors' tyrants and despots.)

CHAPTER 9

THEY MUST BE PERSONS OF TRUTH

1. They are trustworthy and do not willfully break their oaths. They abide by the oath of the office, upholding the Constitution and the laws.
2. They can be relied upon to do the right thing: "to do right to all manner of people without fear or favour, affection or ill-will."[15]
3. They speak the truth and honor their word.
4. They do not follow the behest of the wicked who say, "The words should not agree with the deeds of the diplomat."[16]
5. They do not practice doublespeak.
6. They do not practice making promises that they have no intention of keeping.
7. They do not practice deceit. They do not practice saying one thing when their intention is to mean or do another thing.
8. They are reliable and dependable.
9. They have strong moral and spiritual values.
10. They are not repeatedly proven to be liars in things pertaining to their public stewardship.

Who is fit for public office? Those who are people of truth! Does this mean that the able person who fears God and the person of truth who hates covetousness do not make mistakes? Of course not! There is a big difference between making mistakes and practicing deception.

Someone once said, "Politics has its own morality." [17]

> When the wicked cometh, then cometh
> also contempt and with ignominy reproach.
> (Proverbs 18:3 KJV)

> Ig'nominy, n. [L. ignominia; in and nomen,
> against name or reputation.] Public disgrace;
> shame; reproach; dishonor; infamy. (Noah
> Webster's 1828 Dictionary of American English)

When rulers and/or public officials practice a morality of their own by showing contempt for the rules, norms, and ethical and professional codes of conduct that have been established to preserve order and aid with the good governance of a nation, sooner or later, there will be so much brokenness in the system that both they and the nation they serve will be censured, treated with contempt and disdain, and brought to public shame and disgrace.

Banana republics are the laughingstocks of both the national and international community. That is what corrupt public officials do to nations!

> When you become entitled to exercise the
> right of voting for public officers, let it be
> impressed on your mind that God commands
> you to choose for rulers just men who will
> rule in the fear of God. The preservation of a
> republican government depends on the faithful
> discharge of this duty; if the citizens neglect
> their duty and place unprincipled men in office,
> the government will soon be corrupted; laws

will be made not for the public good so much as for selfish or local purposes; corrupt or incompetent men will be appointed to execute the laws; the public revenues will be squandered on unworthy men; and the rights of the citizens will be violated or disregarded. If a republican government fails to secure public prosperity and happiness, it must be because the citizens neglect the Divine commands and elect bad men to make and administer the laws. When a citizen gives his suffrage [his vote] to a man of known immorality he abuses his trust; he sacrifices not only his own interest, but that of his neighbour; he betrays the interest of his country.[18]

CHAPTER 10

ASSESS YOUR REPRESENTATIVE'S LIKELY PERFORMANCE IN PUBLIC OFFICE

Having examined and studied God's four criteria for assessing the suitability of candidates for public office, we are now in a position to develop a simple weighted rating instrument for objectively assessing candidates and teams of candidates.

I have adapted a simple weighted rating tool developed by Dr. Gary J. Evans, PMP, which is used in project management that electors or leaders can use to objectively assess the suitability of individuals and teams running for public office. I call this adapted tool *Jethro's Integrity Test.*

This is how you use Jethro's Integrity Test to rate candidates and their teams

- To rate your representative, complete the table on the following page.
- Weight factors have already been assigned to each criterion.
- Do not change the weight factors.
- Weight factor significance are as follows:
  1 = not significant
  2 = somewhat significant
  3 = significant
  4 = very significant
  5 = extremely significant

- Enter your score for each criterion and then multiply the score by the weight factor to get a weighted score for each criterion. Then add up all the weighted scores to determine your candidate's overall score.
- Weight factors are whole numbers, usually between 1 and 5, with 1 indicating a rating criterion of low significance and 5 indicating a rating criterion of high significance.
- Rating scores are also numbered between 1 and 5.

Use a rating scale of 1 to 5 to score your candidate:

- 1 = does not meet expectations
- 2 = somewhat meets expectations (or you don't know or are unsure whether expectations are met)
- 3 = meets expectations
- 4 = more than meets expectations
- 5 = greatly exceeds expectations

Notes

- Scores could be stated in multiples of 0.5 if need be for example 2.5. 4.5, 1.5, etc.
- When you are unsure of what score to assign to a criterion for an individual due to lack of information, you should assign a score of 2 (2 = somewhat meets expectations).
- It is a good idea for a family as a unit—or a husband and wife as a unit—to engage in the rating process to include wider perspectives on the candidate's profile in arriving at consensus.

- When assessing a slate of political candidates, it is advisable to begin by assessing the leader of the political Party. The Leader's JIT score will give some indication of the kind of Governance that is likely if his party forms the Government.

How Is Your Representative Likely to Perform in Public Office?

The following table is an example of how the tool is used to rate a single candidate.

Jethro's Integrity Test				
Candidate's Name: John Doe				
Jethro's Criteria	Weight	Score		Weighted Score
Capable	4	2.25		10
Fears God	5	3.5		17.5
Hates Covetousness	5	3		15
Person of Truth	5	3		15
Overall Score				57.5

Scores 51–60: Poor Governance

- The public is very disappointed in the public official's management of the affairs of the state and its resources.
- Their management of state affairs and resources does not meet public expectations.

- There are highly unacceptable levels of wastage of state resources due to very high levels of incompetence and/or corruption.
- There is a loud public outcry accompanied by demonstrations and protests.
- There are widespread public calls for the removal of the public officer.

Appendix B is a blank form that can be copied and used for rating individual candidates.

The following table is an example of how the tool is used to rate a team of four candidates.

Jethro's Integrity Test							
		Individual Team Member (TM) Scores					
Jethro's Criteria	Weight	TM1	TM2	TM3	TM4	Average Score	Weighted Score
Capable	4	5	5	5	5	5	20
Fears God	5	2	4	3	4	3.25	16..25
Hates Covetousness	5	4	4	4	4	4	20
Person of Truth	5	2	4	3	4	3.25	16.25
	Overall Score						72.5

Read appendix A for an interpretation of the overall scores.

Scores 71–80: Good Governance

- Their management of the affairs of the state and its resources meets or exceeds the public's expectations.
- There are tolerable levels of losses to state resources due to good management of project or program risks.
- There are some public concerns about areas that lack accountability.

Instead of using a Microsoft Word Table, Jethro's Integrity Test for teams can be set up in Microsoft Excel where more team members can be added. Also, the calculations could be automated. Setting up JIT in Microsoft Excel also makes the tool more dynamic. It looks like a dashboard in its application.

After candidates are elected to office, more information may come to light about their suitability criteria. If so, their scores on individual criterion can be adjusted to reflect this new information in real time, thus giving an accurate picture of the overall team's likely performance.

Appendix E is a blank form that can be copied and used for rating a team of candidates.

CHAPTER 11

JETHRO'S INTEGRITY TEST

The principles explained in this book, particularly Jethro's Integrity Test, provide you with a tool to assess the suitability of persons who offer themselves for public office. Though some level of subjectivity is involved with the use of this instrument, proper usage of the tool via thorough background checks on candidates soliciting your support will enable you to cut through the political hype, emotions, and other biases and the razzle-dazzle of heavily funded campaign advertising to zero in on the criteria that really matters.

However, in highly developed countries, such as the United States, the front-runners in election campaigns have links to those who own and control the media. Through these links, they often get the media to suppress information about their lives and character, which would otherwise enable the electorate to make more objective assessment about their suitability for public office (based on facts). They also use their links to the mainstream media to propagandize the electorate. They employ public relations and political consulting firms to demonize their opponents on social media. This is a major obstacle.

Independent investigative journalists can greatly assist the electorate by profiling candidates using these criteria. They can help make the assessment of candidates more objective by unearthing relevant information with their superior resources and investigative skills.

The tool is particularly useful in situations that have a mix of suitable and unsuitable candidates. Even in a field of only unsuitable candidates, the tool is still helpful. It removes the element of surprise at the corrupt behavior of public officers and their teams by enabling the electorate to make pretty accurate predictions about their performances. It will also be helpful as an indicator of the level of vigilance that needs to be exercised in monitoring the performances of public officers and politicians and their teams.

The usage of this tool is not restricted to the assessment of candidates running for public office. It can also be used to assist in the screening of leaders in private business and nongovernmental organizations.

CHAPTER 12

EFFECTING CHANGE THROUGH THE PRAYER OF FAITH

In the preceding chapter, we acknowledged the limitations of Jethro's Integrity Test. However, the test will produce very accurate assessments once the relevant information is available.

Journalists, reporters, and the public relations machinery of political parties do not apply all the criteria of JIT when they profile candidates. When you listen to the presentations of candidates at political rallies or conventions, their academic qualifications, work experience, and competence are greatly emphasized. You seldom hear anything stating to what extent they fear God, to what extent they hate covetousness, and to what extent they are people of truth.

This information gap greatly reduces our ability to thoroughly assess candidates. Even if we had perfect information, the pool of candidates offered might not contain any men or women of integrity. So what do we do then? It may seem that we are stuck without a solution and are unable to rid the government of corrupt politicians.

However, the all-wise and all-knowing God is never without a strategy for any eventuality. He has another powerful weapon that can get the job done: the prayer of faith! It is the prayer of faith by righteous people that "makes tremendous power available dynamic in its working" (James 5:16 AMPC). The prayer of faith can change nations:

Casting down imaginations, and every high thing that exalteth itself against the knowledge of God, and bringing into captivity every thought to the obedience of Christ. (2 Corinthians 10:5 KJV)

Elijah was a man with a nature like ours, and he prayed earnestly that it would not rain; and it did not rain on the land for three years and six months. And he prayed again, and the heaven gave rain, and the earth produced its fruit. (James 5:17–18 NKJV)

In many places, including temples, mosques, and churches, many prayers are offered up. Some churches have six to nine hours of "all-night prayer" once or twice a month, which includes earnest and fervent groaning and crying out to God. However, when all is said and done, in many instances, the people really do not believe. How do you know? They are waiting to see the answer to their prayers before they believe and thank God for the thing requested. Many times, they simply pray, forget about the thing requested, and quickly move on to something else. The evidence that people do not believe is the fact that the church does not continually give thanks for the answer to the requests made—even though it is not yet seen.

Paul exhorts the saints to watch and look out for the answers to their prayers with thanksgiving:

Continue in prayer, and watch in the same with thanksgiving. (Colossians 4:2 KJV)

This implies that the church must continually thank God for the things for which they have prayed until the answer is manifested. In the same manner in which a mother would watch for her children to come home from school at the end of the day, the church must watch for the answer to our prayers.

Many people say that we need more prayers. We have had plenty of prayers, but in many instances, they appear to not have been answered. We need more prayers of faith! It is not the abundance of prayers per se that moves God; it is prayers of faith.

Prayers of faith must satisfy at least eight conditions:

1. The prayer must be according to the will of God.

    And this is the confidence that we have in him, that, if we ask any thing according to his will, he heareth us. (1 John 5:14 KJV)

2. Those who have prayed must believe that God has heard their prayers and has granted their requests.

    And if we know that he hear us, whatsoever we ask, we know that we have the petitions that we desired of him. (1 John 5:15 KJV)

3. Those who pray must know with certainty that God will act because He loves us. He is good, and His mercy endures forever!

    Again I say unto you, That if two of you shall agree on earth as touching anything that they shall ask, it shall be done for them of my Father which is in heaven. (Matthew 18:19 KJV)

Therefore I say unto you, What things soever ye desire, when ye pray, believe that ye receive them, and ye shall have them. (Mark 11:24 KJV)

O give thanks unto the Lord, for he is good: for his mercy endureth for ever. Let the redeemed of the Lord say so, whom he hath redeemed from the hand of the enemy. (Psalm 107:1–2 KJV)

4. Those who pray must forgive those who trespass against them.

    And whenever you stand praying, if you have anything against anyone, forgive him, that your Father in heaven may also forgive you your trespasses. (Mark 11:25 NKJV)

    Take heed to yourselves. If your brother sins against you, rebuke him; and if he repents, forgive him. And if he sins against you seven times in a day, and seven times in a day returns to you, saying, "I repent," you shall forgive him. (Luke 17:3–4 NKJV)

5. The corporate body that prayed must continue to give thanks for the thing requested until it is manifested—even if it has not yet been seen.

    Continue in prayer and watch in the same with thanksgiving. (Colossians 4:2 KJV)

6. The prayer must be earnest and fervent. This means crying out unto God and pouring out your heart unto him. Our prayers cannot really be earnest and fervent if we are not burdened with what we are asking for.

    > Confess your faults one to another, and pray one for another, that ye may be healed. The effectual fervent prayer of a righteous man availeth much. (James 5:16 KJV)

7. Those praying must keep the New Covenant by partaking of the Lord's Supper in faith.

    > He that eateth my flesh, and drinketh my blood, dwelleth in me, and I in him. (John 6:56 KJV)

    > If ye abide in me, and my words abide in you, ye shall ask what ye will, and it shall be done unto you. (John 15:7 KJV)

8. The prayer must be prayed by the righteous.

    > The Lord is far from the wicked: but he heareth the prayer of the righteous. (Proverbs 15:29 KJV)

    > Confess your faults one to another, and pray one for another, that ye may be healed. The effectual fervent prayer of a righteous man availeth much. (James 5:16 KJV)

    > The effectual fervent prayer of a righteous man availeth much. (James 5:16 KJV)

The earnest, fervent prayers of the righteous avail much. The prayers of those who believe and know for sure that they are perfectly 100 percent righteous "make tremendous power available dynamic in its working" (James 5:16 AMPC) to make things happen.

The prayers of those who do not know for sure and do not believe with certainty that they are 100 percent perfectly righteous cannot invoke the power of God to effect changes to nations.

If you were to ask most people today, including Christians, if they are righteous, many would answer, "Yes," "I think so," "I am somewhat righteous," or "Frankly, I am not sure."

If you were to ask those who answered yes, why they think they are righteous, they might say, "Well, I don't smoke, I don't commit fornication and adultery, I don't tell lies, I generally don't do bad things, and I try my best to do good things. I generally am a good person"

If you rephrased the question and asked if they were sure they were 100 percent perfectly righteous, they might say, "No, I don't think I am 100 percent perfectly righteous."

If you were to rephrase the question and ask how righteous they are on a scale of 1 to 100 percent, you would probably get a range of answers from around 60 percent or up to 99 percent.

If you were to ask them why they are not 100 percent perfectly righteous, they might say, "Well, you know that the scriptures says, 'There is none righteous' (Romans 3:10 KJV), and we have all fallen short of the glory of God."

People cannot be 50 percent righteous, 60 percent righteous, or 99 percent righteous. They are either 100 percent perfectly righteous or not. There is no in between! Is it possible for anyone to be 100 percent perfectly righteous? Yes! Absolutely! How? It is only by the propitiatory sacrifice and blood of Jesus Christ—not by your good deeds!

If you believe that you are made righteous by your good deeds—not committing adultery, not telling lies, and generally not doing bad things—you are grossly mistaken.

> But we are all as an unclean thing, and all our righteousness are as filthy rags; and we all do fade as a leaf; and our iniquities, like the wind, have taken us away. (Isaiah 64:6 KJV)

So how does one become 100 percent perfectly righteous? Paul the Apostle explains:

> Therefore by the deeds of the law there shall no flesh be justified in his sight: for by the law is the knowledge of sin. But now the righteousness of God without the law is manifested, being witnessed by the law and the prophets; Even the righteousness of God which is by faith of Jesus Christ unto all and upon all them that believe: for there is no difference: For all have sinned, and come short of the glory of God; Being justified freely by his grace through the redemption that is in Christ Jesus: Whom God hath set forth to be a propitiation through faith in his blood, to declare his righteousness for the remission of sins that are past, through the forbearance of God; To declare, I say, at this time his righteousness: that he might be just, and the justifier of him which believeth in Jesus. Where is boasting then? It is excluded. By what law? Of

works? Nay: but by the law of faith. Therefore we
conclude that a man is justified by faith without
the deeds of the law. (Romans 3:20–28 KJV)

To be justified means to be imputed with God's righteousness,
which includes being made free from the guilt of sin, being
blessed, being made holy and blameless and irreproachable in
God's sight, and cleansing of all of your sins by the blood of
Jesus Christ. Let's listen to the Apostle Paul again:

> Even as David also describeth the blessedness
> of the man, unto whom God imputeth
> righteousness without works, Saying, "Blessed
> are they whose iniquities are forgiven, and
> whose sins are covered. Blessed is the man to
> whom the Lord will not impute sin." (Romans
> 4:6–8 KJV)

> And you, that were sometime alienated and
> enemies in your mind by wicked works, yet
> now hath he reconciled in the body of his
> flesh through death, to present you holy and
> unblameable and unreproveable in his sight.
> (Colossians 1:21–22 KJV)

Therefore, a person is made 100 percent perfectly righteous by
being imputed with God's righteousness, which is when they
believe in Jesus Christ as their Lord and Savior. When they
believe in Jesus's propitiatory sacrifice—that Jesus Christ died
on the cross at Calvary and shed His blood for all of our sins,
past, present, and future—they are remitted, forgiven, and gone
forever!

> For Christ is not entered into the holy places made with hands, which are the figures of the true; but into heaven itself, now to appear in the presence of God for us: Nor yet that he should offer himself often, as the high priest entereth into the holy place every year with blood of others; For then must he often have suffered since the foundation of the world: but now once in the end of the world hath he appeared to put away sin by the sacrifice of himself. (Hebrews 9:24–26 KJV)

It is not your moral rectitude that makes you righteous; it is your faith in the propitiatory sacrifice of Jesus Christ for you. Righteousness is not an honor or status that is earned or obtained by your good deeds; it is a gift from God. It is the gift of all God's blessings. Can your good deeds earn you all God's blessings, including eternal life? Of course not!

> But not as the offence, so also is the free gift. For if through the offence of one many be dead, much more the grace of God, and the gift by grace, which is by one man, Jesus Christ, hath abounded unto many. And not as it was by one that sinned, so is the gift: for the judgment was by one to condemnation, but the free gift is of many offences unto justification. For if by one man's offence death reigned by one; much more they which receive abundance of grace and of the gift of righteousness shall reign in life by one, Jesus Christ.) Therefore as by the offence of one judgment came upon all men to condemnation;

even so by the righteousness of one the free gift came upon all men unto justification of life. (Romans 5:15–18 KJV)

For if Abraham were justified by works, he hath whereof to glory; but not before God. For what saith the scripture? Abraham believed God, and it was counted unto him for righteousness. Now to him that worketh is the reward not reckoned of grace, but of debt. But to him that worketh not, but believeth on him that justifieth the ungodly, his faith is counted for righteousness. (Romans 4:2–5 KJV)

Cometh this blessedness then upon the circumcision only, or upon the uncircumcision also? For we say that faith was reckoned to Abraham for righteousness. How was it then reckoned? When he was in circumcision, or in uncircumcision? Not in circumcision, but in uncircumcision. And he received the sign of circumcision, a seal of the righteousness of the faith which he had yet being uncircumcised: that he might be the father of all them that believe, though they be not circumcised; that righteousness might be imputed unto them also. (Romans 4:9–11 KJV)

This last passage of scripture teaches that righteousness refers to the blessing of God that is imputed to the believer. That blessing is imputed to the believer when they believe in Jesus as their Savior. At that point, all their sins are forgiven, blotted out, and washed away by the blood of Jesus. They are gone forever.

When he had by himself purged our sins, sat down on the right hand of the Majesty on high. (Hebrews 1:3 KJV)

For this is the covenant that I will make with the house of Israel after those days, saith the Lord; I will put my laws into their mind, and write them in their hearts: and I will be to them a God, and they shall be to me a people: And they shall not teach every man his neighbour, and every man his brother, saying, Know the Lord: for all shall know me, from the least to the greatest. For I will be merciful to their unrighteousness, and their sins and their iniquities will I remember no more. (Hebrews 8:10–12 KJV)

This is the covenant that I will make with them after those days, saith the Lord, I will put my laws into their hearts, and in their minds will I write them; And their sins and iniquities will I remember no more. (Hebrews 10:16–17 KJV)

Note, however, that this forgiveness is not a license to commit sin! Many people interpret the word *righteousness* to mean moral rectitude. Moral rectitude is self-righteousness. Instead, the righteousness of God refers to the sum total of God's blessings, which includes freedom from the guilt of sin.

So only your unwavering belief that you have been justified, made totally free from the guilt of all sin for all time, and therefore blessed by God made perfectly 100 percent righteous by the righteousness of God, which he imputes to you when you believe on Jesus the Christ as your Lord and Savior, makes you righteous and qualifies you to pray the prayer of faith.

> The Lord is far from the wicked: but he heareth the prayer of the righteous. (Proverbs 15:29 KJV)

> The sacrifice of the wicked is an abomination to the Lord: but the prayer of the upright) is his delight. (Proverbs 15:8 KJV)

> In this passage, "upright" refers to the righteous. The psalms teach us that the upright refers to the righteous:

> Be glad in the Lord, and rejoice, ye righteous: and shout for joy, all ye that are upright in heart. (Psalm 32:11 KJV)

> Rejoice in the Lord, O ye righteous: for praise is comely for the upright. (Psalm 33:1 KJV)

CHAPTER 13

CONTENDING WITH THE POWERS OF DARKNESS THROUGH THE PRAYER OF FAITH

> Finally, my brethren, be strong in the Lord, and in the power of his might. Put on the whole armour of God that ye may be able to stand against the wiles of the devil. For we wrestle not against flesh and blood, but against principalities, against powers, against the rulers of the darkness of this world, against spiritual wickedness in high places.
>
> **—Ephesians 6:10–12 (KJV)**

In this passage, the apostle Paul informs us that our battle against evil is not really with people. Even though humans are the faces we put on these evils, they are the unseen, highly intelligent, and extremely powerful evil beings, principalities, powers, rulers of the darkness of this world, and evil and wicked spirits in high places.

These evil spirits and their cohorts are responsible for influencing the evil and wickedness, including corruption, that is taking place around the world. These demonic powers are assigned to destroy and corrupt all that is good and pure on the face of the earth.

Most people, including many Christians, are acutely unaware of the existence and modus operandi of these evil powers.

As a result, they blame, contend with, and direct their fights against earthly organizations and individuals in their efforts to thwart their works. In such instances, they end up beating the air. Carnal efforts—conferences, debates, public protests, and legislative efforts—will not and cannot by themselves deter evil spirits from carrying out their wicked works. You cannot wage war against evil spirits with carnal weapons.

The apostle Paul speaks of standing against "the wiles of the devil." A wile is "a trick or stratagem practiced for ensnaring or deception; a sly, insidious artifice" (Noah Webster's 1828 *Dictionary of American English*).

These demonic powers are masters of deception, trickery, treachery, craft, cunning, and sorcery. As fallen angels that were cast out of heaven with Satan, they have thousands of years of experience in manipulating and deceiving humans into carrying out their evil, mischief, and wickedness on earth.

One of their first acts of deception is to make people think they do not exist. In fact, some people know of their existence because these persons invoke their assistance to obtain influence, promotion, fame, and power to inflict harm and injuries to their enemies.

Secondly, they make people think they do not meddle in the affairs of the states and nations. They employ stratagems to cause people to think other people are their enemies and are the real cause of evil in our society. We cannot withstand their stratagems and shenanigans except with the spiritual weapons provided to us by our Lord and Savior Jesus Christ.

The apostle Paul says in withstanding these evil powers, we are not to depend on the power of our own carnal weapons. Instead, we are to rely and depend upon the power of God's might: the supernatural, mighty, wonder working, miracle power of God.

This is where many people miss the mark. To the carnal mind, it is easier to believe in the strength of politicians, their political parties, systems, and organizations, and other expressions of human strength, such as the military, to change things than it is to believe in the power of God in heaven.

> Finally, my brethren, be strong in the Lord, and in the power of his might. (Ephesians 6:10 KJV)

I am not implying that God does not use people or organizations or institutions to execute His will on earth. God continues to work through humans, institutions, and organizations. However, disciples of the Lord Jesus Christ are admonished not to rely only on the strength of humanity. Instead, we should put our trust in, rely upon, and depend upon the power of God's might to battle these unseen spiritual forces of darkness.

> It is better to trust in the Lord than to put confidence in man. It is better to trust in the Lord than to put confidence in princes. (Psalm 118:8–9 KJV)

> After this manner therefore pray ye: Our Father which art in Heaven, Hallowed be thy name. Thy kingdom come, Thy will be done in earth, as it is in Heaven. Give us this day our daily bread. And forgive us our debts, as we forgive our debtors. And lead us not into temptation, but deliver us from evil: For thine is the kingdom, and the power, and the glory, forever. Amen. (Matthew 6:9–13 KJV)

In this prayer, Jesus teaches us that we must rely on the Father's divine power to lead us away from temptation and to deliver us from evil. Temptation here refers to the human propensity to commit lawlessness and wickedness. Evil here refers to that which is harmful and hurtful to the mind, body, soul, and spirit. They will rob us of our peace, prosperity, safety, and security.

In this prayer, Jesus is implying that all that is good that we would like to have on this earth can only be accomplished through the divine power of our Father in heaven.

Notice the implied emphasis on the Father's power to accomplish these things:

He brings the kingdom to earth:

> Thy kingdom come. (Matthew 6:10 KJV)

His will is to be done on earth—not ours:

> Thy will be done in earth, as it is in heaven. (Matthew 6:10 KJV)

His power provides our daily bread:

> Give us this day our daily bread. (Matthew 6:11 KJV)

His power forgives sins:

> And forgive us our debts, as we forgive our debtors. (Matthew 6:12)

His power restrains us from practicing lawlessness:

> And lead us not into temptation. (Matthew
> 6:13 KJV)

His power delivers us from evil:

> But deliver us from evil. (Matthew 6:13 KJV)

We must acknowledge that the kingdom is His, the power to accomplish all these things is His, and He must get the glory:

> For thine is the kingdom, and the power, and the
> glory. (Matthew 6:13 KJV)

As strong as we think we are—and as powerful as we think earthly organizations are—it takes the power of God to restrain lawlessness and advance that which is good in the earth. Crime is a major problem in many nations. Governments are spending billions of dollars on national security and training, and they are arming their security forces to the teeth. Despite this, the dam that has been restraining lawlessness seems to be cracking under the pressure of society's evils. Hundreds of thousands of body bags are in store right now, waiting for those who will die through violence in our cities and communities, in wars, civil unrest, and violent street protests.

Governments, cities, and communities are losing the battle against lawlessness. Manufacturers and sellers of guns, ammunition, and security systems are cashing in on people's fear of criminals and of one another. We have relied solely on the strength and counsel of others and on science and technology. We have become our own gods:

> Put not your trust in princes, nor in the son of
> man, in whom there is no help. (Psalm 146:3 KJV)

> No king is saved by the multitude of an army; a
> mighty man is not delivered by great strength.
> A horse is a vain hope for safety; neither shall it
> deliver any by its great strength. Behold, the eye
> of the Lord is on those who fear Him, on those
> who hope in His mercy (Psalm 33:16–18 NKJV)

In the Lord's Prayer, Jesus teaches us that a seemingly simple thing as having bread on our tables requires the intervention of the Father's divine power.

Those who are very rich and powerful might be shocked at this statement. They might say, "If I want a loaf of bread, there are numerous bakeries from which I can order a loaf! As a matter of fact, I can buy the bakery that bakes the bread—with cash, right now—if I wished to!"

However, have you given thought to how the wheat grain originated and reproduced? If God revoked the seed-bearing and other reproductive power of all plants, animals, and sea creatures, how many more years do you think humans would be able to survive on earth with all our technology? If God withdrew all the oxygen in the atmosphere for ten minutes, I wonder if only the poor, the working class, and the middle class would die and the rich and powerful 1 percent would survive.

Jesus taught us how to end the Lord's Prayer:

> For thine is the kingdom, and the power and the
> glory, forever. Amen. (Matthew 6:13 KJV)

At the end of the Lord's Prayer, we must acknowledge that all good things on the earth—in our families, our communities, and our nations—only are done by His divine power. Yes, the power to produce these seemingly simple things comes from the Father in heaven—and only from Him.

Who made the air that we breathe? Who made the life in our bodies?

The next time you say grace before a meal to give thanks for the food provided, end your prayer by saying:

> For thine is the kingdom, and the power and the
> glory, forever. Amen. (Matthew 6:13 KJV)

Many of our leaders (religious as well as secular), teachers, scholars, intellectuals, and ordinary people in the street have forgotten this truth. When the books are opened in heaven at the end of time, the records may very well show that the reason nations descended into decadence was because people ceased praying this simple prayer—or its equivalent—in faith.

Only God's divine power can thwart the human propensity for lawlessness and the onslaught of the powers of darkness that beset us daily. Change can be effected in our nation by continually praying the prayer of faith for our nation and its leaders:

> First of all, supplications, prayers, intercessions,
> and giving of thanks, be made for all men; For
> kings, and for all that are in authority; that
> we may lead a quiet and peaceable life in all
> Godliness and honesty. For this is good and
> acceptable in the sight of God our Savior. (1
> Timothy 2:1–3 KJV)

We must lift up the leaders of our nations with individual names and pray the prayer of faith for their salvation and conversion. Our prayers have been too general.

Yes, we are to pray something like this:

> Father God, we lift up Mayor John Doe before you right now and ask You to save his soul. We ask You to pull down every high thing in his life that exalts itself against the knowledge of God and bring into captivity every thought of his to the obedience of Christ.

Lift up your members of the Houses of Representatives, congressmen, mayors, governors, state and senate representatives, local government councilors, and heads of state, agencies, and ministries by their individual names. We must also pray the prayer of faith for other prominent people.

In the scripture quoted above, the root meaning of the Greek word translated "authority" is *prominence*:

> Prominent: Standing out so as to be seen easily; conspicuous; particularly noticeable [Dictionary.com]

Prominent people occupy high office and are part of officialdom, but they also include the business elite, celebrities, attorneys, the judiciary, members of chambers of commerce, newspaper columnists, bloggers, journalists, and athletes. All prominent people stand out!

However, prominent people also include criminals. They stand out in our local communities and nationally. The elite, the rich, and the powerful influence the drafting and passage of many of the laws enacted in our nations.

You will appreciate the importance of praying for prominent people when you learn that the Supreme Court of the United States of America has ruled that same-sex marriage is legal in all fifty states in America, and the House of Commons and Lords in the United Kingdom has ruled that same-sex marriage is now legal in England and Wales. Some prominent politicians belong to secret societies where members must perform vile acts as part of their initiations.

Fifty years ago, legalizing same-sex marriage could have never happened because many politicians and judges still had the fear of God in their hearts. A new generation of the elite has arisen! A new generation of MPs, congressmen, and judges have not been affected by the Gospel, and their hearts have not been converted. As a result, we have enacted laws that permit ungodly practices in the two most powerful nations of the world. Those societies were founded on Judeo-Christian teachings and values, and their missionaries evangelized the world.

We are also to pray that God's will be done in our nations and in their institutions as it is in heaven:

> Father God, we lift up the ministry of [name of ministry] before you right now, and we ask that thy will be done in the ministry of [name of ministry], that you will cause our ministry [name of ministry] to be managed according to thy will in heaven.

God desires His will to be done in the earth—and not the will of you or me or some politician. If our prayers are for His will to be done in the affairs of the state, then He will act. He told us how to pray:

Thy will be done on earth as it is in heaven.
(Matthew 6:10 KJV)

God does not follow the agenda of mayors or governors whose wisdom is finite. Politicians cannot know with certainty what will happen in the next five minutes—much less for the next five years.

We definitely cannot be taken seriously if we expect the creator of the heavens and the earth to follow the agenda of mortal men. When we are praying for our nations and their institutions, let us remember to say: "Thy will be done on earth, in our nation and in our institutions of state as it is in heaven."

We elect the politicians and leave it entirely up to them to transform our nation. We expect them and the institutions they manage to solve crimes. We expect them to solve the problems with the economy. We expect them to plan and develop the nation. We expect them to unite the people. We expect them to solve the problems in our schools and with our youths. We expect them to eradicate all of society's ills. We expect them to effectively integrate all that is promised in their manifestos and bring them to pass while we sit back and wait to see what will happen next. Many of them genuinely believe that passing certain bills will eliminate many of the ills of society.

When things don't turn out as expected, we blame the government and demand change. We change the government, but things remain the same. We didn't get change; we got exchange!

We fail to realize that—even with all the credentials behind their names and their years of experience—politicians and their technocrats are mere humans. We naïvely expect these individuals—with their finite human wisdom, limited strength, and fallen human nature—to master the mammoth complexities of the infrastructural, social, economic, cultural, developmental, and spiritual transformation of our nations.

The Lord warns us what will happen when we put our trust in the strength of humans and not in Him:

> Thus says the Lord: "Cursed is the man who trusts in man and makes flesh his strength, whose heart departs from the lord. for he shall be like a shrub in the desert, and shall not see when good comes, but shall inhabit the parched places in the wilderness, in a salt land which is not inhabited." (Jeremiah 17:5–6 NKJV)

To be cursed means to be cut off from; to be separated from; to be alienated from God's blessings; to be cut off from all that is good.

The Lord counsels us as to what will happen when we put our trust in Him and not in the strength of humans:

> Blessed is the man who trusts in the Lord, and whose hope is the Lord. For he shall be like a tree planted by the waters, which spreads out its roots by the river, and will not fear when heat comes; but its leaf will be green, and will not be anxious in the year of drought, nor will cease from yielding fruit. (Jeremiah 17:7–8 NKJV)

To be blessed means to have God's goodness and mercy follow you all the days of your life and to be given all that pertains to life and godliness:

> Put not your trust in princes, nor in the son
> of man, in whom there is no help. His breath
> goeth forth, he returneth to his earth; in that
> very day his thoughts perish. Happy is he that
> hath the God of Jacob for his help, whose hope
> is in the Lord his God: Which made Heaven,
> and earth, the sea, and all that therein is:
> which keepeth truth for ever: Which executeth
> judgment for the oppressed: which giveth food
> to the hungry. The Lord looseth the prisoners.
> (Psalm 146:3–7 KJV)

God continues to use humans to execute His will on earth, but He exhorts us that our reliance, dependence, and trust must always be in Him and not in the instrument He is using. So we must continue to pray in faith: "Thy will be done in earth and in our government and its institutions as it is in heaven."

By doing so, we invoke the unseen, mighty, wondrous, miracle-working power of God to intervene in the affairs of our nations. How is He going to intervene? What will He do? Where will He start? I don't know—but we don't need to know! God is omnipotent and omniscient. In scripture, God says:

> For my thoughts are not your thoughts, neither
> are your ways my ways, saith the Lord. For as
> the Heavens are higher than the earth, so are my
> ways higher than your ways, and my thoughts
> than your thoughts. (Isaiah 55:8–9 KJV)

Because God is infinite and people are finite, don't expect God to think the way you think or act the way you act. You are limited in your intelligence, and your conclusions and initiatives are based on evidence that is seen. Your strength is limited; therefore, the actions you can take are limited.

God intelligence is infinite and His conclusions and actions are based on the abundance of evidence that is seen and unseen. You are constrained by the forces in and of this world. God is sovereign! God can do exceedingly and abundantly above what you can think or ask. Therefore, all we need to do is humble ourselves, put our trust in God, pray, and watch for the changes with thanksgiving!

CHAPTER 14

THE COUP DE GRÂCE

By the blessing of the upright the city is exalted:
but it is overthrown by the mouth of the wicked.
—Proverbs 11:11 (KJV)

Death and life are in the power of the tongue: and
they that love it shall eat the fruit thereof.
—Proverbs 18:21 (KJV)

These scriptures give great insight into the impact and consequences of our speech. The first thing that we notice is that God has placed the destiny of our nations squarely in the mouths of the upright (the righteous). He has delegated to the upright (the righteous) the authority to transform their nation, and that authority is in their mouths.

Notice the scripture does not say that we are to ask God to bless our nation. It says we who are upright (righteous) must do the blessing. We are to use our mouths to decree blessings over our nations, and our nations will be exalted. Whatever the righteous decree over their nations determines what they will become. If we speak death (all that is contrary to God's goodness) in our nations, that is what will come forth:

> With all the criminal activity that exists in this
> country, I can't see things getting any better.
> Things will only get worse! This nation is in a

complete mess, and I don't think anything can
be done to reverse it.

When we speak like that, we can expect decline and decadence
because we spoke it!

> A good man out of the good treasure of his heart
> bringeth forth that which is good; and an evil
> man out of the evil treasure of his heart bringeth
> forth that which is evil: for of the abundance of
> the heart his mouth speaketh. (Luke 6:45 KJV)

> Keep thy heart with all diligence; for out of it are
> the issues of life. Put away from thee a froward
> mouth, and perverse lips put far from thee.
> (Proverbs 4:23–24 KJV)

We will speak whatever we feed our minds, hearts, and spirits.
If we feed our hearts with that which is negative, perverse, and
contrary to the goodness and righteousness of God, that is what
we will speak—and that is what will come to pass. Conversely,
if we speak that which is according to God's goodness and
righteousness, that is what will come to pass.

In the scripture above, the word *perverse* does not mean that
which is obscene, as many of us think. It means that which is
contrary to the truth, the righteousness of God, and what God has
declared. The power to invoke good or evil—and life or death—
resides in the tongue, but it is the heart that informs the tongue.

Good things will come forth in our nations when the
righteous take the time to bless their nations and speak good
and well of them. When we speak life (all that is according to
God's righteousness and goodness), that is what will come forth.

If we were to say, "Our nation is blessed, and the goodness of Jehovah God prevails over our land," then good will prevail over evil because the righteous spoke it.

You might ask, "How can that be? It's impossible! Things have gone too far!"

> Jesus said unto him, "If thou canst believe, all things are possible to him that believeth." (Mark 9:23 KJV)

> And Jesus looking upon them saith, "With men it is impossible, but not with God, for with God all things are possible." (Mark 10:27 KJV)

I have been taught not to doubt what God says even if it seems impossible or foolish to me. With God, nothing shall be impossible! Is anything too hard for God to do? The problem is that we think it is by human strength that such mammoth transformation will be accomplished. God uses humans, but His will gets done by the Power of His Might

> Great is our Lord, and of great power: his understanding is infinite. He delighteth not in the strength of the horse: he taketh not pleasure in the legs of a man. The Lord taketh pleasure in them that fear him, in those that hope in his mercy. (Psalm 147:5–11 KJV)

To fear God simply means to put your trust in Him, to depend upon Him, and to rely upon Him because of His exceedingly great love for us and His omnipotence and omniscience.

God's mercy refers to the miraculous and awesome deeds

of loving-kindness and goodwill He performs for the benefit of those who put their trust in Him.

In the Lord's Prayer, Jesus taught us that it is the Father's divine power that accomplishes His will on earth.

To bless means "to speak well of; to proclaim a benediction." God is saying that the upright (the righteous)—through the simple act of speaking words of blessings over their nations— can invoke His divine power to bring transformation to the lives of a people and their land and cause them to excel, to be lifted up above other nations, to be models of all that is good and noble for other nations:

- in spiritual riches: love, joy, peace, longsuffering, gentleness, goodness, faith, meekness, and temperance
- in the health and longevity of our citizens
- in the decency and civicmindedness of its citizens
- in wealth and the prosperity of individual citizens and their families (spiritually and materially)
- in the provision of excellent health and human and social services
- in national security (maintenance of peace and freedom from internal strife, conflicts, human trafficking, drug trafficking, and other criminal activities)
- in the military
- in international reputation and rank
- in economic development
- as leaders in all spheres of human endeavor

These scriptures reveal that it is what the righteous confess with their mouths over their nations that determines whether it is exalted or suffers reproach.

By the blessing of the upright the city is exalted:
but it is overthrown by the mouth of the wicked.
(Proverbs 11:11 KJV)

Have we taken this injunction seriously? I don't think so! Instead of responding to the spiritual and moral decay in our nations with negative pronouncements, we ought to bless them. Blessing our nations does not mean that we cannot acknowledge their failures. However, whatever we confess with our mouths—good or bad—will determine their destinies.

These scriptures reveal that when the righteous begin to bless their nations, they will be transformed. Our problem has been *mauvaise langue* (bad tongue) and unbelief! Much of what we believe and confess about our nations is informed by the scandalmongering of our "town criers" in the news media, social media, and the repeated propaganda of vested interests.

The town criers in the news media and social media have legitimate roles in our society, but we need to distinguish between their scandalmongering and the truth.

Scandalmongering here refers to the negative pronouncements that are made about a nation's or state's destiny. These pronouncements are often contrary to the truth, contrary to the will of God, and contrary to the righteousness (blessedness) of God.

Many of us eagerly tune into our favorite radio and TV talk shows every day to listen to what the town criers are saying. Many of them are esteemed expert analysts. Some make positive pronouncements, but many more paint a negative picture of a rough road ahead, hardship, belt tightening, increasing crime, job cuts, internecine conflicts, and uncertainty. These pronouncements can leave many of us bewildered, frightened, and confused. Not surprisingly, echoing what the naysayers have said, we can end up in a state of doubt, anxiety, and uncertainty about the future. These town criers can also come in the form of psychics who make all sorts of predictions; some are good, but most are gloomy.

We certainly need to be concerned about the pronouncements of the naysayers. We need to understand that the negative pronouncements of the naysaying town criers will come to pass if the righteous remain silent.

Edmund Burke (1729–1797) said, "All that is necessary for evil to triumph is for good men to do nothing."[19]

I believe all that is necessary for evil to triumph is for righteous men to not bless their nations. If the righteous will awaken to their callings, tune in to heaven's injunctions, and obey the injunction to bless their nations, the naysayers' pronouncements will be annulled. The blessing of the righteous will invoke God's power, which will prevail over the naysayers' pronouncements and effect change for the good in our nations.

The town criers may say, "The economy is bad, revenues from gas and oil are falling, and things will only get worse." However, the righteous in faith (those who believe in God's Word) will decree, "Our nation is blessed, and the goodness of Jehovah God prevails over our nation!" God's goodness will prevail over our nation, and things will improve:

> Trust in the Lord with all thine heart; and lean not unto thine own understanding. In all thy ways acknowledge him, and he shall direct thy paths. (Proverbs 3:5–6 KJV)

Those who are disciples of Jesus Christ are not to draw conclusions and predicate initiatives solely on the basis of our understanding or the reports of expert analysts. We are to trust in, rely on, and depend on God. How does this apply in practice? Let us return to the statements of our town criers:

> The economy is bad, revenues from gas and oil
> prices are falling; things will only get worse.

This conclusion could be based on very sound economic and financial analysis by the most erudite experts in the field. However, it is the conclusion of mere men and women with limited intelligence. Their profession does not incorporate the loving-kindness (the Kheh-sed)[20] of God or the miraculous and awesome deeds of goodwill that He performs for the benefit of His beloved. The experts do not have the final say. The experts do not have the final say!

An excellent example from scripture is the nation of Egypt in the days when Joseph, the son of Jacob, was one of its princes. The Pharaoh had a dream about an imminent seven-year famine that threatened to ruin Egypt's economy—and the world's economy. The prescience of the dream was confirmed by a young man called Joseph who was gifted in the interpretation of dreams; Pharaoh's own counselors were not able to interpret the dream. Pharaoh sought a solution to this impending national disaster.

Recognizing the gift on the young man's life, Pharaoh proceeded to appoint Joseph to the position of governor over Egypt, second-in-command only to Pharaoh himself with the mandate to implement a solution to avert the impending national disaster.

Joseph's recommendation was that Egypt should set aside, annually, 20 percent of its national grain production in the seven years leading up to the famine. This store of grain would be used to meet Egypt's consumption needs during the seven years of famine. The Egyptians did as Joseph recommended, and the collapse of their economy was averted.

Economists might say, "What is so great about Joseph's recommendation? A twelfth grader could have figured that out. Furthermore, where is the evidence of the miraculous and awesome works of God's goodwill in all of this?"

Joseph's recommendations and the math might have been simple, but the miracle is what God did to Egypt's grain production in the seven years leading up to the start of the famine under Joseph's stewardship. God made the grain fields of Egypt abound so much in grain production that the annual 20 percent savings over seven years met Egypt's total consumption needs for seven years of the famine—and the consumption needs of the world for the duration of the famine:

> Joseph gathered very much grain, as the sand of the sea, until he stopped counting, for it was immeasurable. (Genesis 41:49 NKJV)

> And the seven years of famine began to come, as Joseph had said. The famine was in all lands, but in all the land of Egypt there was bread. So, when all the land of Egypt was famished, the people cried to Pharaoh for bread. Then Pharaoh said to all the Egyptians, "Go to Joseph; whatever he says to you, do." The famine was over all the face of the earth, and Joseph opened all the storehouses and sold to the Egyptians. And the famine became severe in the land of Egypt. So all countries came to Joseph in Egypt

to buy grain, because the famine was severe in
all lands. (Genesis 41:54–57 NKJV)

That is called the mercy (Kheh-sed)[21] or the loving-kindness of
God: the miraculous and awesome deeds of goodwill that He
performs for the benefit of His beloved.

The miracles performed by God were twofold. He
orchestrated the ascendancy to high office of a just man—a man
of uncanny wisdom—and He miraculously increased Egypt's
grain production under the stewardship of this just man. What
he has done with grain, he can do with oil and gas and any other
valuable national resource if we believe!

God prefers to work such miracles with just rulers who
rule in the fear of God. The sovereign God is omniscient, and
omnipotent, and He knows all things and with whom nothing
is impossible. He can do exceedingly abundantly above all that
we can think or ask:

Trust in the Lord with all thine heart; and lean
not unto thine own understanding. (Proverbs
3:5 KJV)

As disciples of Christ, we are not to draw conclusions and
initiate actions based solely on our understanding or the reports
of the so-called experts.

While the town criers are complaining, the righteous
will put our trust in God and act in faith in response to His
injunction: "Our nation is blessed, and the goodness of Jehovah
God prevails over our nation!"

Jesus answered and said unto them, "Verily I say
unto you, If ye have faith, and doubt not, ye shall

> not only do this which is done to the fig tree, but also if ye shall say unto this mountain, Be thou removed, and be thou cast into the sea; it shall be done. And all things, whatsoever ye shall ask in prayer, believing, ye shall receive." (Matthew 21:21–22 KJV)

> Nevertheless when the Son of man cometh, shall he find faith on the earth? (Luke 18:8 KJV)

We must have faith in God, confidence in His love for us, and patience. We must patiently endure. We must remain calm and composed without complaint while waiting for God to deliver us from the adversities we face.

Many of us quit when nothing happens after praying five or six times. We give up! We stop watching for the manifestation of the thing we requested or decreed. We conclude that maybe it is not God's will for the thing to take place. This was not the attitude of the prophet Elijah when God told him that He would send rain upon the land of Israel after three years of drought:

> And it came to pass after many days, that the word of the Lord came to Elijah in the third year, saying, Go, shew thyself unto Ahab; and I will send rain upon the earth. (1 Kings 18:1 KJV)

Elijah went up to Mount Carmel and prayed that the rains God promised would come. However, nothing happened after he prayed the first time. He prayed again, and nothing happened. He prayed again four more times, and nothing happened

However, being confident that God cannot lie and that He God always performs His Word, Elijah continued to pray and watch. He did not quit; he remained calm and composed. He was fully convinced that God would do what He had promised to do. On the seventh occasion, a small cloud appeared in the sky, indicating the onset of rain:

> And Elijah said unto Ahab, Get thee up, eat and drink; for there is a sound of abundance of rain. So Ahab went up to eat and to drink. And Elijah went up to the top of Carmel; and he cast himself down upon the earth, and put his face between his knees, And said to his servant, Go up now, look toward the sea. And he went up, and looked, and said, There is nothing. And he said, Go again seven times. And it came to pass at the seventh time, that he said, Behold, there ariseth a little cloud out of the sea, like a man's hand. And he said, Go up, say unto Ahab, Prepare thy chariot, and get thee down, that the rain stop thee not. And it came to pass in the mean while, that the heaven was black with clouds and wind, and there was a great rain. And Ahab rode, and went to Jezreel. (1 Kings 18:41–45 KJV)

> Elias was a man subject to like passions as we are, and he prayed earnestly that it might not rain: and it rained not on the earth by the space of three years and six months. And he prayed again, and the heaven gave rain, and the earth brought forth her fruit. (James 5:17–18 KJV)

When seeking God for the showers of blessings, we have to exercise faith and patient endurance. In waiting for the showers of blessings to manifest, we may have to endure the drought for a season that may seem to us to be an inordinately long time.

God heard Elijah the very first time he prayed, but God—for His sovereign reason—chose to delay the time when the rain would begin falling. With God, delay does not mean denial! Maybe God was simply testing Elijah's faith. The moral is that the timing of the manifestation of God's answers to our prayers is not always in sync with the time when we expect it to happen.

The blessings of God miraculously descending upon a land and its people transform that nation. The mighty, wondrous, miracle-working power of God enabled Egypt to thwart a national disaster.

In the light of all that has been revealed so far in this chapter, we really do not qualify to complain about our nation's failures and its poor governance if we are not continually decreeing blessings over our nation in obedience to God's injunction to bless our nation. From time to time, some people say, "God bless our nation!" Even our leaders occasionally say it at the end of their addresses to the nation. Do we really have faith in what we say—or do we wish for the best when we make such statements.

There is a difference. Has the saying become more of a cliché than a confession of faith? I am not necessarily questioning the sincerity of our leaders and other persons who make such statements, but I am trying to make the point that it is the faith in the statement that really matters and not the wish. When people make these statements, do they really believe God has heard us and will act in response to the decrees—or do we wish He would act?

To wish is not an act of faith because it is mixed with uncertainty about the outcome. To have faith is to be certain or be assured of the outcome because it is God's will. God expects us to make such decrees in faith because He has given His Word that he will act in response to it. However, if we don't have faith in what we decree, there is very little likelihood that it will come to pass:

> But without faith it is impossible to please him: for he that cometh to God must believe that he is, and that he is a rewarder of them that diligently seek him. (Hebrews 11:6 KJV)

CHAPTER 15

RIGHTEOUSNESS EXALTS A NATION

Righteousness exalteth a nation: but sin is a reproach to any people.

—Proverbs 14:34 (KJV)

In the previous chapter, I explained what it means for a nation to be exalted. This scripture reveals that it is the blessings of God miraculously descending upon a land and its people that transform that nation.

In this passage, *righteousness* refers to the blessings of God. Many people interpret the word to mean moral rectitude, and they interpret the passage to mean that if people can by their own efforts live morally upright lives, our nations will be blessed and exalted. This fallacy has resulted in much frustration, futility, and hypocrisy in people's lives.

The righteousness referred to in this passage is the righteousness of God and refers to the sum total of God's blessings. The righteousness (blessing) of God descending on the people of a nation and its land exalts that nation. The righteousness (blessing) of God descending on an individual enables them to live right. This interpretation makes perfect sense because we know—from our own experiences and history—that no one has been able to live a morally perfect life since Adam sinned.

Truth shall spring out of the earth; and
righteousness shall look down from Heaven.
Yea, the Lord shall give that which is good; and
our land shall yield her increase. (Psalm 85:11–
12 KJV)

Therefore, a nation's excellence does not come by people's efforts
to live right, but by the blessing of God. The righteousness
(blessings) of God being imputed to individuals or a nation
enables them to live right. Man's attempt at moral rectitude is
human self-righteousness. It is not the righteousness of God.

In rich and developed countries, some people might
argue that we are already blessed because we have excelled
economically and in science, technology, the arts, sports, and
culture. That might be so in some instances, but in many
instances, the truth is hidden beneath the glitz and glamour
of the neon lights. In many countries, the truth is echoed in
Jesus's statement:

Because thou sayest, I am rich, and increased
with goods, and have need of nothing; and
knowest not that thou art wretched, and
miserable, and poor, and blind, and naked.
(Revelation 3:17 KJV)

These words of Jesus—given by revelation to the apostle John
about the church at Laodicea in the first century—also apply to
many churches today. If Jesus says that about His church, how
much more applies to the rest of society?

This is not meant to condemn the citizens of rich and
developed countries. How can I condemn those Jesus loves and
those He came to save?

> For God so loved the world that he gave his only begotten Son, that whosoever believeth in him should not perish, but have everlasting life. For God sent not his Son into the world to condemn the world; but that the world through him might be saved. He that believeth on him is not condemned: but he that believeth not is condemned already, because he hath not believed in the name of the only begotten Son of God. (John 3:16–18 KJV)

The angels who appeared to the shepherds in the field on the night of the Savior's birth echoed the truth that Jesus came to save and not to condemn:

> And the angel said unto them, "Fear not: for, behold, I bring you good tidings of great joy, which shall be to all people. For unto you is born this day in the city of David a Savior, which is Christ the Lord. And this shall be a sign unto you; ye shall find the babe wrapped in swaddling clothes, lying in a manger. And suddenly there was with the angel a multitude of the Heavenly host praising God, and saying, Glory to God in the highest, and on earth peace, good will toward men." (Luke 2:8–14 KJV)

What does this peace and goodwill mean? Isaiah the prophet explained it when he prophesied of Jesus's ministry:

> The Spirit of the Lord God is upon me; because the Lord hath anointed me to preach good tidings unto the meek; he hath sent me to bind

up the brokenhearted, to proclaim liberty to the captives, and the opening of the prison to them that are bound; To proclaim the acceptable year of the Lord, and the day of vengeance of our God; to comfort all that mourn; To appoint unto them that mourn in Zion, to give unto them beauty for ashes, the oil of joy for mourning, the garment of praise for the spirit of heaviness; that they might be called trees of righteousness, the planting of the Lord, that he might be glorified. (Isaiah 61:1–3 KJV)

At the start of His ministry, Jesus confirmed Isaiah's prophecy:

And he came to Nazareth, where he had been brought up: and, as his custom was, he went into the synagogue on the sabbath day, and stood up for to read. And there was delivered unto him the book of the prophet Esaias. And when he had opened the book, he found the place where it was written, The Spirit of the Lord is upon me, because he hath anointed me to preach the gospel to the poor; he hath sent me to heal the brokenhearted, to preach deliverance to the captives, and recovering of sight to the blind, to set at liberty them that are bruised, To preach the acceptable year of the Lord. And he closed the book, and he gave it again to the minister, and sat down. And the eyes of all them that were in the synagogue were fastened on him. And he began to say unto them, This day is this scripture fulfilled in your ears. (Luke 4:16–21 KJV)

The "poor" mentioned in this scripture refers to the spiritually poor and not the materially poor.

Jesus came to repair our broken lives and our broken relationships with the Father. There is so much brokenness in our lives today. Marriages are broken, family relationships are broken, people's health and wealth are broken, and in many cases, their minds are broken. Almost everyone now sees a psychiatrist or psychotherapist, and even the psychiatrists see their own psychotherapists.

Love for one another and for our fellow human beings has grown cold:

> And because lawlessness will abound, the love of many will grow cold. (Matthew 24:12 NKJV)

However, the truth about our dire brokenness is hidden behind the facades of our material possessions. Jesus came to heal the brokenhearted and free all who were blighted by the curse of sin, physical and spiritual sickness and disease, material poverty, strife, spiritual poverty or emptiness, the guilt of sin, and other societal ills that have held people captive for centuries. In a nutshell, Jesus came to set us free:

> If the Son therefore shall make you free, ye shall be free indeed. (John 8:36 KJV)

> Behold, I stand at the door, and knock: if any man hear my voice, and open the door, I will come in to him, and will sup with him, and he with me. (Revelation 3:20 KJV)

That's the voice of a loving, gentle, and caring Savior. That is perfect politeness. He loves us and wants to share His peace with us—but only with our permission. He will never force His will on us. He has the love and humility to leave His throne of majesty in glory to come to our doors on earth and knock. Which earthly monarch will leave his palace and go to the door of a commoner and knock so that he could sit with him, sup with him, and share in his morsel of bread? If we reject the Savior's love, then we have only ourselves to blame if we find ourselves eternally separated from God and lost in eternal torments at the end of time.

Jesus in speaking to the apostle John, the revelator, was simply giving a reality check to the Church. And this is what I have done by quoting Jesus's statement: I have given a reality check for what is happening in our nations. It is what it is! Our nations are overwhelmed with sin and reproach. Our cities and communities are swamped with vile affections—just as it was in the apostle Paul's day:

> For this cause God gave them up unto vile affections: for even their women did change the natural use into that which is against nature: And likewise also the men, leaving the natural use of the woman, burned in their lust one toward another; men with men working that which is unseemly, and receiving in themselves that recompence of their error which was meet. And even as they did not like to retain God in their knowledge, God gave them over to a reprobate mind, to do those things which are not convenient; Being filled with

all unrighteousness, fornication, wickedness, covetousness, maliciousness; full of envy, murder, debate, deceit, malignity; whisperers, backbiters, haters of God, despiteful, proud, boasters, inventors of evil things, disobedient to parents, without understanding, covenant breakers, without natural affection, implacable, unmerciful. (Romans 1:26–31 KJV)

In the ages before Christ came to die for the sins of humanity, God became so frustrated with human sin, rebellion, and contempt for Him, His Goodness, and His loving-kindness that He gave the people over to a reprobate (corrupt, debased, immoral) mind, to do those things that are not convenient.

The apostle Paul, speaking in the book of Romans, of those reprobates, said:

Who knowing the judgment of God, that they which commit such things are worthy of death, not only do the same, but have pleasure in them that do them. (Romans 1:32 KJV)

Though the reprobates were worthy of death for being so sinful and corrupt, the scripture says:

For God so loved the world, that He gave his only begotten Son, that whosoever believeth in him should not perish, but have everlasting life. For God sent not his Son into the world to condemn the world; but that the world through him might be saved. (John 3:16–17 KJV)

It is only the love of God expressed through the propitiatory sacrifice of Jesus Christ for the remission of sins and the power of His blessing that can save humanity from the curse of sin:

> For I am not ashamed of the gospel of Christ: for it is the power of God unto salvation to everyone that believeth; to the Jew first, and also to the Greek. For therein is the righteousness of God revealed from faith to faith: as it is written, the just shall live by faith. (Romans 1:16–17 KJV)

Yes! Why should I or anyone be ashamed of the loving-kindness, power, and blessing of God? It delivers us from the sin, shame, and reproach that has contaminated our lives, translates us into the marvelous light of Jesus Christ, and imputes His blessings and eternal life to us.

CHAPTER 16

BE A PART OF THE SOLUTION AND NOT THE PROBLEM

You may be a king, a president a prime minister, a governor, a mayor, or another high-ranking public official. You may be genuinely concerned about the onerous blight that is called corruption in your nation and government. You may have been wondering what can be done to stem this burdensome tide of malfeasance and crookedness. This book has given you insight into the cause of the problem and its solutions.

You have seen that the solution lies in electing rulers of integrity to public office, praying the prayer of faith that those in prominence will believe in Jesus Christ as Lord and Savior, blessing your nation, and praying that God's will be done in your government, your nation, and its institutions—as it is in heaven.

As a leader, you cannot have true integrity and pray the prayer of faith, invoking the power of God to bring change to your nation if you are not imputed with the righteousness of God. Yes! I say imputed! As I explained in the previous chapter, righteousness is a gift of all God's blessings. It is imputed to a person when they accept Jesus Christ as their Lord and Savior, believe in the propitiatory sacrifice of Jesus Christ, and believes that Jesus Christ died on the cross at Calvary and shed His blood so that all of his sins—past, present, and future—are remitted, forgiven, blotted out completely, and gone forever!

Righteousness is not a standing of right or acceptance before

God that is earned by your good deeds; it is a gift from God. It is the gift of all of His blessings, and it is irrevocable, immutable, and invariable!

> For the gifts and calling of God are without repentance. (Romans 11:29 KJV)

> Every good gift and every perfect gift is from above, and cometh down from the Father of lights, with whom is no variableness, neither shadow of turning. (James 1:17 KJV)

God will never revoke the gift of His righteousness. He has imputed it to you for as long as you continue to trust in Jesus as your Savior. His righteousness never lapses, it never ceases, and it never comes to an end. It endures forever!

> I will betroth you to Me forever; yes, I will betroth you to Me in righteousness and justice, in loving-kindness and mercy. (Hosea 2:19 NKJV)

> His seed shall be mighty upon earth: the generation of the upright shall be blessed. Wealth and riches shall be in his house: and his righteousness endureth for ever. (Psalm 112:2–3 KJV)

You can, however, choose to give up the blessing by renouncing Jesus Christ. This righteousness (blessedness) is constant, and it does not vary with the magnitude of your good deeds or miserable failures. In other words, you are not less righteous today because you made some bad mistakes and did some terrible things. You were not more righteous yesterday because you did some good deeds and avoided doing wrong things. Your righteousness endures forever. The blood of Jesus Christ purges and cleanses you of all of your sins—past, present, and future.

> For Christ is not entered into the holy places made with hands, which are the figures of the true; but into heaven itself, now to appear in the presence of God for us: Nor yet that he should offer himself often, as the high priest entereth into the holy place every year with blood of others; For then must he often have suffered since the foundation of the world: but now once in the end of the world hath he appeared to put away sin by the sacrifice of himself. And as it is appointed unto men once to die, but after this the judgment: So Christ was once offered to bear the sins of many; and unto them that look for him shall he appear the second time without sin unto salvation. (Hebrews 9:24–28 KJV)

> God, who at various times and in various ways spoke in time past to the fathers by the prophets, has in these last days spoken to us by His Son, whom He has appointed heir of all things, through whom also He made the worlds; who being the brightness of His glory and the express image of His person, and upholding all things by the word of His power, when He had by Himself purged our sins, sat down at the right hand of the Majesty on high. (Hebrews 1:1–3 NKJV)

This is the covenant that I will make with them after those days, saith the Lord, I will put my laws into their hearts, and in their minds will I write them; And their sins and iniquities will I remember no more. Now where remission of these is, there is no more offering for sin. (Hebrews 10:16–18 KJV)

You may say that you can understand how your past sins can be forgiven, but you find difficulty understanding how your future sins—though not yet committed—can be forgiven in the present! It is not difficult to comprehend if you understand the concept of *diplomatic immunity* or *sovereign immunity*.

According to freedictionary.com, *diplomatic immunity* is:

A principle of international law that provides foreign diplomats with protection from legal action in the country in which they work. Established in large part by the Vienna conventions, diplomatic immunity is granted to individuals depending on their rank and the amount of immunity they need to carry out their duties without legal harassment. Diplomatic immunity allows foreign representatives to work in host countries without fully understanding all the customs of that country. However, diplomats are still expected to respect and follow the laws and regulations of their host countries; immunity is not a license to commit crimes.

If a person with immunity is alleged to have committed a crime or faces a civil lawsuit, the department of state alerts the government that the diplomat works for. The Department of State also asks the home country to waive immunity of the alleged offender so that the complaint can be moved to the courts. If immunity is not waived, prosecution cannot be undertaken. [22]

According to freedictionary.com, *sovereign immunity* is:

> The legal protection that prevents a sovereign state or person from being sued without consent. Sovereign immunity is a judicial doctrine that prevents the government or its political subdivisions, departments, and agencies from being sued without its consent. The doctrine stems from the ancient English principle that the monarch can do no wrong.[23]

When you believe on the Lord Jesus Christ as your Lord and Savior for the remission of your sins, you are given legal protection in heaven that is analogous to diplomatic or sovereign immunity. I call it the believer's immunity.

My definition of the believer's immunity is as follows:

> A principle of divine grace; a gift of God's grace that provides all disciples of the Lord Jesus Christ with protection from legal action in heaven, arising out of any sin, wrongdoing, or offense they commit while on earth.
>
> Established by heaven's decree, "the believers' immunity" is granted to the disciples of the Lord Jesus Christ, first to deliver them from eternal condemnation, and to allow them

to serve the Lord Jesus Christ without divine legal harassment.

Believer's immunity allows disciples of the Lord Jesus Christ to serve Him here on earth without fully understanding all of heaven's customs and the customs of their host countries. However, disciples of Christ are still expected to respect and follow heaven's laws and the laws and regulations of their host countries.

The scriptures teach that, as believers, we have immunity from sin:

> Even as David also describeth the blessedness of the man, unto whom God imputeth righteousness without works, Saying, Blessed are they whose iniquities are forgiven, and whose sins are covered. Blessed is the man to whom the Lord will not impute sin. (Romans 4:6–8 KJV)

> Blessed is he whose transgression is forgiven, whose sin is covered. Blessed is the man to whom the Lord does not impute iniquity, and in whose spirit there is no deceit. (Psalm 32:1–2 NKJV)

Immunity, however, is not a license to practice sin:

> Dearly beloved, I beseech you as strangers and pilgrims, abstain from fleshly lusts, which war against the soul; Having your conversation honest among the Gentiles: that, whereas they

speak against you as evildoers, they may by your good works, which they shall behold, glorify God in the day of visitation. Submit yourselves to every ordinance of man for the Lord's sake: whether it be to the king, as supreme; Or unto governors, as unto them that are sent by him for the punishment of evildoers, and for the praise of them that do well. For so is the will of God, that with well doing ye may put to silence the ignorance of foolish men: As free, and not using your liberty for a cloke of maliciousness, but as the servants of God. (1 Peter 2:11–16 KJV)

What shall we say then? Shall we continue in sin, that grace may abound? God forbid. How shall we, that are dead to sin, live any longer therein? (Romans 6:1–2 KJV)

It is interesting to note that scripture refers to the disciples of Christ as "ambassadors for Christ" (2 Corinthians 5:20 KJV).

If earthly governments understand the need for their diplomats to have immunity so that they can be free to perform their duties without legal harassments, how much more does the kingdom of heaven understand the need for ambassadors for Christ to have immunity so they too can be free to perform their duties without legal harassments in serving Christ?

How much more shall the blood of Christ, who through the eternal Spirit offered himself without spot to God, purge your conscience from dead works to serve the living God? (Hebrews 9:14 KJV)

People whose consciences are burdened with the guilt of sin are unable to joyfully and effectively serve God. Serving with God requires genuine faith. Persons whose consciences are not completely free from the guilt of sin cannot exercise genuine faith.

God cannot employ such individuals to work along with Him in executing righteousness, justice, and loving-kindness and to perform great exploits in the earth so that His name is glorified. Only those whose consciences have been purged from dead works (sin) can serve the living God. Are humans wiser than God—or did we get this wisdom from God?

All disciples of the Lord Jesus Christ have the believer's immunity, but most of them do not know it! A significant difference between diplomatic immunity and the believers' immunity is that whereas nations may sometimes waive the diplomat's immunity, heaven never waives the believer's immunity except when the person has fallen away by rejecting the Savior after having believed:

> Moreover whom he did predestinate, them he also called: and whom he called, them he also justified: and whom he justified, them he also glorified. What shall we then say to these things? If God be for us, who can be against us? He that spared not his own Son, but delivered him up for us all, how shall he not with him also freely give us all things? Who shall lay anything to the charge of God's elect? It is God that justifieth. Who is he that condemneth? It is Christ that died, yea rather, that is risen again, who is even at the right hand of God, who also maketh intercession for us. (Romans 8:30–34 KJV)

Who shall lay anything to the charge of God's elect? This means that no one—not even God— can bring a formal charge of the guilt of any sin in heaven's court against the disciple of Jesus Christ. If such is attempted, it will not be entertained! It will immediately be struck down!

The disciple has the believer's immunity, and God never waives the believer's immunity. The propitiation through the shed blood of Jesus is so efficacious that it blots out all sins—past, present, and future—forever!

So, having been imputed with the righteousness of God and with the believer's immunity, what would that do for you and your relationship with God if you became a disciple of Jesus Christ?

You would have the boldness and confidence to approach God and talk to Him. That means you do not allow yourself to feel guilty, ashamed, disgraced, embarrassed, unworthy, humiliated, or inferior to go into God's presence because of your sins. All of your sins are annulled and washed away by the blood of Jesus. There is nothing to feel ashamed about before God. You are His child. You are a king and a priest to Him. You have the believer's immunity:

> Having therefore, brethren, boldness to enter into the holiest by the blood of Jesus, By a new and living way, which he hath consecrated for us, through the veil, that is to say, his flesh; And having an high priest over the house of God; Let us draw near with a true heart in full assurance of faith, having our hearts sprinkled from an evil conscience, and our bodies washed with pure water. Let us hold fast the profession of our

faith without wavering; (for he is faithful that promised;) And let us consider one another to provoke unto love and to good works. (Hebrews 10:19–24 KJV)

And they sung a new song, saying, Thou art worthy to take the book, and to open the seals thereof: for thou wast slain, and hast redeemed us to God by thy blood out of every kindred, and tongue, and people, and nation. (Revelation 5:9 KJV)

You are always in right standing with God. God can never point a condemning finger at you and charge you with being guilty of any sin because all your sins have been annulled and washed away by the blood of Jesus.

What shall we then say to these things? If God be for us, who can be against us? He that spared not his own Son, but delivered him up for us all, how shall he not with him also freely give us all things? Who shall lay any thing to the charge of God's elect? It is God that justifieth. Who is he that condemneth? It is Christ that died, yea rather, that is risen again, who is even at the right hand of God, who also maketh intercession for us. Who shall separate us from the love of Christ? shall tribulation, or distress, or persecution, or famine, or nakedness, or peril, or sword? (Romans 8:31–35 KJV)

For Christ is not entered into the holy places made with hands, which are the figures of the true; but into heaven itself, now to appear in the presence of God for us: Nor yet that he should offer himself often, as the high priest entereth into the holy place every year with blood of others; For then must he often have suffered since the foundation of the world: but now once in the end of the world hath he appeared to put away sin by the sacrifice of himself. And as it is appointed unto men once to die, but after this the judgment: So, Christ was once offered to bear the sins of many; and unto them that look for him shall he appear the second time without sin unto salvation. (Hebrews 9:24–28 KJV)

You have direct access to God's throne and the boldness to talk to God, anytime, anywhere, and about anything.

Having therefore, brethren, boldness to enter into the holiest by the blood of Jesus, By a new and living way, which he hath consecrated for us, through the veil, that is to say, his flesh; And having an high priest over the house of God; Let us draw near with a true heart in full assurance of faith, having our hearts sprinkled from an evil conscience, and our bodies washed with pure water. Let us hold fast the profession of our faith without wavering (for he is faithful that promised) and let us consider one another to provoke unto love and to good works: (Hebrews 10:19–24 KJV)

You are blessed with *all* spiritual blessings.

Blessed be the God and Father of our Lord Jesus Christ, who hath blessed us with all spiritual blessings in heavenly places in Christ. (Ephesians 1:3 KJV)

You lack nothing!

For in him dwelleth all the fulness of the Godhead bodily. And ye are complete in him, which is the head of all principality and power. (Colossians 2:9–10 KJV)

You are given the right to be a son of God and joint heir with Christ.

But as many as received him, to them gave he power to become the sons of God, even to them that believe on his name. (John 1:12 KJV)

For ye are all the children of God by faith in Christ Jesus. For as many of you as have been baptized into Christ have put on Christ. There is neither Jew nor Greek, there is neither bond nor free, there is neither male nor female: for ye are all one in Christ Jesus. And if ye be Christ's, then are ye Abraham's seed, and heirs according to the promise. (Galatians 3:26–29 KJV)

The Spirit itself beareth witness with our spirit, that we are the children of God: And if children, then heirs; heirs of God, and joint-heirs with

Christ; if so be that we suffer with him, that we may be also glorified together. (Romans 8:16–17 KJV)

God the father exalts you to the status of a king, and priest in His kingdom.

John to the seven churches which are in Asia: Grace be unto you, and peace, from him which is, and which was, and which is to come; and from the seven Spirits which are before his throne; And from Jesus Christ, who is the faithful witness, and the first begotten of the dead, and the prince of the kings of the earth. Unto him that loved us, and washed us from our sins in his own blood, And hath made us kings and priests unto God and his Father; to him be glory and dominion for ever and ever. Amen. (Revelation 1:4–6 KJV)

And they sung a new song, saying, Thou art worthy to take the book, and to open the seals thereof: for thou wast slain, and hast redeemed us to God by thy blood out of every kindred, and tongue, and people, and nation; And hast made us unto our God kings and priests: and we shall reign on the earth. (Revelation 5:9–10 KJV)

God looks upon you with delight and great pleasure. He delights in you.

But God, who is rich in mercy, for his great love wherewith he loved us, Even when we were dead in sins, hath quickened us together with Christ, (by grace ye are saved;) And hath raised us up together, and made us sit together in heavenly places in Christ Jesus: (Ephesians 2:4–6 KJV)

But to the saints that are in the earth, and to the excellent, in whom is all my delight. (Psalm 16:3 KJV)

The Lord taketh pleasure in them that fear him, in those that hope in his mercy. (Psalm 147:11 KJV)

You have been redeemed (delivered) from every curse.

Christ hath redeemed us from the curse of the law, being made a curse for us: for it is written, Cursed is every one that hangeth on a tree: That the blessing of Abraham might come on the Gentiles through Jesus Christ; that we might receive the promise of the Spirit through faith. (Galatians 3:13–14 KJV)

You have received the gift of God's righteousness (freedom from the guilt of sins and His Blessings), His manifold gifts of loving-kindness, tender mercies, compassion, and the irrevocable riches of His goodness.

Nevertheless death reigned from Adam to Moses, even over them that had not sinned after the similitude of Adam's transgression, who is the figure of him that was to come. But not as the offence, so also is the free gift. For if through the offence of one many be dead, much more the grace of God, and the gift by grace, which is by one man, Jesus Christ, hath abounded unto many. And not as it was by one that sinned, so is the gift: for the judgment was by one to condemnation, but the free gift is of many offences unto justification. For if by one man's offence death reigned by one; much more they which receive abundance of grace and of the gift of righteousness shall reign in life by one, Jesus Christ. (Romans 5:14–17 KJV)

You have been perfected and made righteous forever. Yes! Forever!

But this man, after he had offered one sacrifice for sins for ever, sat down on the right hand of God; From henceforth expecting till his enemies be made his footstool. For by one offering he hath perfected for ever them that are sanctified. Whereof the Holy Ghost also is a witness to us: for after that he had said before, This is the covenant that I will make with them after those days, saith the Lord, I will put my laws into their hearts, and in their minds will I write them; (Hebrews 10:12–16 KJV)

You will receive the Gift of His Holy Spirit.

Then Peter said unto them, Repent, and be baptized every one of you in the name of Jesus

> Christ for the remission of sins, and ye shall
> receive the gift of the Holy Ghost. (Act 2:38 KJV)

> In whom ye also trusted, after that ye heard the
> word of truth, the gospel of your salvation: in
> whom also after that ye believed, ye were sealed
> with that holy Spirit of promise, Which is the
> earnest of our inheritance until the redemption
> of the purchased possession, unto the praise of
> his glory. (Ephesians 1:13–14 KJV)

Again, having been imputed with the righteousness of God, the
believer's immunity, and the gift of the Holy Spirit, you are now
prepared to be part of the solution. By virtue of the blessing of
God upon your life and the gift of His Holy Spirit and having
the integrity of Jesus Christ imputed to you, you will be a person
who can now pray the prayer of faith.

The eyes of the Lord run to and fro throughout the whole
earth, looking for people like you to promote to or function in
leadership positions in your nation:

> When the righteous are in authority, the people
> rejoice: but when the wicked beareth rule, the
> people mourn. (Proverbs 29:2 KJV)

> When it goeth well with the righteous, the city
> rejoiceth: and when the wicked perish, there is
> shouting. (Proverbs 11:10 KJV)

If you want to make a difference by being a man or woman
imputed with the integrity of Christ and being able to pray
the prayer of faith "that makes tremendous power available

dynamic in its working" (James 5:16 AMPC), then you need to have your sins remitted and have the righteousness of God imputed to you and be equipped with the believer's immunity by believing in the Lord Jesus Christ as your Savior who saves you from condemnation to the eternal fires of hell because of your sins.

You can receive the gift and blessing of God's forgiveness, the righteousness of God, the believer's immunity, and the gift of the Holy Spirit right now by praying this simple prayer:

> Father in heaven, I acknowledge that I have been born a sinner, and I have broken your laws, and sinned against You.
>
> I acknowledge that because You are a holy and just God, and if my sins are not forgiven, I must appear before You, in the judgment, to account for my sins when the books, with the record of my sins, are opened.
>
> Lord, today I have learned, that if I believe in Your Son Jesus Christ as my Savior, You will grant me an eternal pardon by forgiving me of all of my sins—past, present, and future—and that my name will be written in the Lamb's Book of Life.
>
> Father, this evening/morning, I confess that:
>
> - I believe in my heart that Jesus is the Christ, the Savior of the world.
> - I believe in my heart that Jesus the Christ came and died and sacrificed His life and shed His Blood so that I could

receive the forgiveness and remission of all of my sins.

- I believe in my heart that Jesus was crucified on the cross at Calvary, was buried and rose from the dead on the third day.

I now take Jesus Christ, as my Lord and my Savior, and believe in Him, for the forgiveness and remission of all of my sins.

Lord Jesus, I thank You for saving me from eternal damnation and from being cast into the lake, which burns with fire, which is the second death.

I thank you, Lord Jesus, for having given unto me, the gift of eternal life, and for writing my name, in the Lamb's Book of Life.

Lord Jesus, I accept Your gift to me of eternal life and salvation.

But what does it say? The word is near you, in your mouth and in your heart" (that is, the word of faith which we preach): that if you confess with your mouth the Lord Jesus and believe in your heart that God has raised Him from the dead, you will be saved. (Romans 10:8–9 NKJV)

For with the heart one believes unto righteousness, and with the mouth confession is made unto salvation. For the Scripture says, "Whoever believes on Him will not be put to shame." (Romans 10:10–11 KJV)

> For there is no distinction between Jew and Greek, for the same Lord over all is rich to all who call upon Him. For "whoever calls on the name of the Lord shall be saved." (Romans 10:12–13 KJV)

If you prayed the above prayer from your heart, then all you need to do next to be obedient to the Lord's command concerning your salvation is to be baptized. (it is to have one's whole body immersed in water. It is not sprinkling).

> And he said unto them, Go ye into all the world, and preach the gospel to every creature. He that believeth and is baptized shall be saved; but he that believeth not shall be damned. (Mark 16:15-16 KJV)

What does it mean to be saved?
First it means to be delivered from being punished with everlasting destruction from the presence of the Lord because of sins.
The scripture says:

> And to you who are troubled rest with us, when the Lord Jesus shall be revealed from heaven with his mighty angels, In flaming fire taking vengeance on them that know not God, and that obey not the gospel of our Lord Jesus Christ: Who shall be punished with everlasting destruction from the presence of the Lord, and from the glory of his power; (2Thessalonians 1:7-9 KJV)

Secondly, it means to be given the gift of eternal life; to be resurrected at the return of the Lord Jesus, and to be taken up into the heavens to live with him and other believers in the new heavens and the new earth.

The scriptures say:

> For the Lord himself shall descend from heaven with a shout, with the voice of the archangel, and with the trump of God: and the dead in Christ shall rise first: Then we which are alive and remain shall be caught up together with them in the clouds, to meet the Lord in the air: and so shall we ever be with the Lord. (1Thessalonians 4:16-17 KJV)

> Behold, I shew you a mystery; We shall not all sleep, but we shall all be changed, In a moment, in the twinkling of an eye, at the last trump: for the trumpet shall sound, and the dead shall be raised incorruptible, and we shall be changed. (1Corinthians 15:51-52 KJV)

> And I saw a new heaven and a new earth: for the first heaven and the first earth were passed away; and there was no more sea. And I John saw the holy city, new Jerusalem, coming down from God out of heaven, prepared as a bride adorned for her husband. And I heard a great voice out of heaven saying, Behold, the tabernacle of God is with men, and he will dwell with them, and they shall be his people, and God himself shall

> be with them, and be their God. And God shall
> wipe away all tears from their eyes; and there
> shall be no more death, neither sorrow, nor
> crying, neither shall there be any more pain:
> for the former things are passed away. And he
> that sat upon the throne said, Behold, I make
> all things new. And he said unto me, Write: for
> these words are true and faithful. (Revelations
> 21:1-5 KJV)

Do not become apprehensive now because you have been invited to confess Jesus Christ as your Lord and Savior and be water baptized. You are not the first and only person or high-ranking public official to have done so.

When the church started in the first century, many high-ranking public officials accepted Jesus as Lord and Savior. They accepted His propitiatory sacrifice for their sins and the blessing that comes with it. The treasury secretary or finance minister of Ethiopia under Candace, queen of Ethiopia in the first century, accepted Jesus as his Savior and was baptized.

> And the angel of the Lord Spake unto Philip,
> saying, Arise, and go toward the south unto
> the way that goeth down from Jerusalem unto
> Gaza, which is desert. And he arose and went:
> and, behold, a man of Ethiopia, an eunuch
> of great authority under Candace queen of
> the Ethiopians, who had the charge of all her
> treasure, and had come to Jerusalem for to
> worship, Was returning, and sitting in his
> chariot read Esaias the prophet. Then the Spirit
> said unto Philip, Go near, and join thyself to

this chariot. And Philip ran thither to him, and heard him read the prophet Esaias, and said, Understandest thou what thou readest? And he said, how can I, except some man should guide me? And he desired Philip that he would come up and sit with him. The place of the scripture which he read was this, He was led as a sheep to the slaughter; and like a lamb dumb before his shearer, so opened he not his mouth: In his humiliation his judgment was taken away: and who shall declare his generation? For his life is taken from the earth. And the eunuch answered Philip, and said, I pray thee, of whom speaketh the prophet this? of himself, or of some other man? Then Philip opened his mouth, and began at the same scripture, and preached unto him Jesus. And as they went on their way, they came unto a certain water: and the eunuch said, See, here is water; what doth hinder me to be baptized? And Philip said, If thou believest with all thine heart, thou mayest. And he answered and said, I believe that Jesus Christ is the Son of God. And he commanded the chariot to stand still: and they went down both into the water, both Philip and the eunuch; and he baptized him. (Acts 8:26–38 KJV)

A centurion, a man of high military rank in the Roman Empire in the first century, accepted Jesus as his Savior and was baptized.

Then Peter went down to the men which were sent unto him from Cornelius; and said,

Behold, I am he whom ye seek: what is the cause wherefore ye are come? And they said, Cornelius the centurion, a just man, and one that feareth God, and of good report among all the nation of the Jews, was warned from God by an holy angel to send for thee into his house, and to hear words of thee. Then called he them in, and lodged them. And on the morrow Peter went away with them, and certain brethren from Joppa accompanied him. And the morrow after they entered into Caesarea. And Cornelius waited for them, and had called together his kinsmen and near friends. And as Peter was coming in, Cornelius met him, and fell down at his feet, and worshipped him. But Peter took him up, saying, Stand up; I myself also am a man. And as he talked with him, he went in, and found many that were come together. And he said unto them, ye know how that it is an unlawful thing for a man that is a Jew to keep company, or come unto one of another nation; but God hath shewed me that I should not call any man common or unclean. Therefore came I unto you without gainsaying, as soon as I was sent for: I ask therefore for what intent ye have sent for me? And Cornelius said, Four days ago I was fasting until this hour; and at the ninth hour I prayed in my house, and, behold, a man stood before me in bright clothing, and said, Cornelius, thy prayer is heard, and thine alms are had in remembrance in the sight of God.

Send therefore to Joppa, and call hither Simon, whose surname is Peter; he is lodged in the house of one Simon a tanner by the sea side: who, when he cometh, shall speak unto thee. Immediately therefore I sent to thee; and thou hast well done that thou art come. Now therefore are we all here present before God, to hear all things that are commanded thee of God. Then Peter opened his mouth, and said, of a truth I perceive that God is no respecter of persons: But in every nation he that feareth him, and worketh righteousness, is accepted with him. The word which God sent unto the children of Israel, preaching peace by Jesus Christ: (he is Lord of all) That word, I say, ye know, which was published throughout all Judaea, and began from Galilee, after the baptism which John preached; How God anointed Jesus of Nazareth with the Holy Ghost and with power: who went about doing good, and healing all that were oppressed of the devil; for God was with him. And we are witnesses of all things which he did both in the land of the Jews, and in Jerusalem; whom they slew and hanged on a tree: Him God raised up the third day, and shewed him openly; Not to all the people, but unto witnesses chosen before of God, even to us, who did eat and drink with him after he rose from the dead. And he commanded us to preach unto the people, and to testify that it is he which was ordained of God to be the Judge of quick and dead. To him give all the prophets' witness that through his name whosoever believeth in him shall receive remission of sins. While Peter yet spake these words, the Holy Ghost fell on all them which heard the word. And they of the circumcision which believed were astonished, as many as came with Peter, because that on the Gentiles also was poured out the gift of the Holy Ghost. For they heard them speak with tongues, and magnify God. Then answered Peter, Can any man forbid water, that these should not be baptized, which have received the Holy Ghost as well as we? And he commanded them to be baptized in the name of the Lord. Then prayed they him to tarry certain days. (Acts 10:21–48 KJV)

A high-ranking official sometimes has to battle their ego and pride in submitting to God. Sometimes they ask, "What will my friends and family say! They will say I have gone nuts! No! I cannot do this, I will be looked upon as a fool, as being weak, as being a Bible-toting fanatic."

Then said Jesus unto his disciples, If any man will come after me, let him deny himself, and take up his cross, and follow me. (Matthew 16:24 KJV)

Following Jesus does not come without reproach. You see, the disciple of Christ is really not of this world. Just as the elite in Jesus's day misunderstood Him, so will the elite in your sphere misunderstand you,

Your colleagues may snub you, your friends may snicker and

laugh at you behind your back, your spouse and children may say that you have gone nuts, you may no longer be welcomed at the boys' or girls' club, or you may no longer be considered for that prominent position that was earmarked for you.

When you tell your friends and family that you have believed on Jesus Christ as your Savior, they will say, "You what? You believe in Jesus! Have you gotten caught up in that religious mumbo jumbo! What has happened to you lately? You know what this will do to your career and to our family! You need to rethink this decision!"

> And every one that hath forsaken houses, or brethren, or sisters, or father, or mother, or wife, or children, or lands, for my name's sake, shall receive an hundredfold, and shall inherit everlasting life. (Matthew 19:29 KJV)

This is the cross you must bear to be free. Thanks be to God that bearing the cross does come with great rewards. Jesus bore His cross—and you must bear yours if you are to be set free:

> Looking unto Jesus the author and finisher of our faith; who for the joy that was set before him endured the cross, despising the shame, and is set down at the right hand of the throne of God. For consider him that endured such contradiction of sinners against himself, lest ye be wearied and faint in your minds. Ye have not yet resisted unto blood, striving against sin. (Hebrews 12:2–4 KJV)

Yes, you too must consider Christ Jesus as you ponder this decision. Jesus bore the cross because of "the joy that was set before Him" (Hebrews 12:2 KJV). He knew about the great benefit His crucifixion, death, burial, and resurrection would bring to humankind.

He despised the shame that was meted out to him. Being confident in Himself as Lord and Christ, being full of compassion and love for sinful humans, not willing that any should perish, and being confident in His mission and purpose and the blessings, the riches of God's goodness and grace that will accrue to humankind through His sacrificial death, He endured the shame and reproach. He refused to allow the hate, the contempt, the ridicule, the threat of violent death, and the venomous hostility by the Jewish mob and Roman soldiers to dissuade him from His mission. For this, He was rewarded with a seat at the right hand of the Father.

You also must be prepared to despise the shame that will attend your decision for the greater benefit, freedom, and blessings it will bring to you and your family and friends—and even those who will persecute you. However, I can guarantee you that when you have been set free, these same people would be seeking you out privately for help with their problems in life. You will be the one they will turn to for comfort, spiritual guidance, and support

> By faith Moses, when he was come to years, refused to be called the son of Pharaoh's daughter; choosing rather to suffer affliction with the people of God, than to enjoy the pleasures of sin for a season; esteeming the reproach of Christ greater riches than the treasures in Egypt: for he

had respect unto the recompence of the reward.
(Hebrews 11:24–26 KJV)

The second chapter of Exodus contains more details about Moses's exile from Egypt.

Matthew was a tax collector in Israel; it was a very lucrative and respected position in the Roman Empire:

> And as Jesus passed forth from thence, he saw a man, named Matthew, sitting at the receipt of custom: and he saith unto him, "Follow me." And he arose, and followed him. (Matthew 9:9 KJV)

> And after these things he went forth, and saw a publican, named Levi, sitting at the receipt of custom: and he said unto him, "Follow me." And he left all, rose up, and followed him. (Luke 5:27–28 KJV)

Zacchaeus was a wealthy tax collector, and he may have acquired his wealth through a mix of hard work and extortion. Zacchaeus lived in Israel during the days of Jesus's ministry. Having heard about Jesus and His love for the people, His loving-kindness, the miracles of goodwill that He performed for the needy and less fortunate, and the encouraging and uplifting words He spoke, Zacchaeus was curious to see and meet with Him.

> And, behold, there was a man named Zacchaeus, which was the chief among the publicans, and he was rich. And he sought to see Jesus who he was; and could not for the press, because he was little of stature. And he ran before, and climbed

up into a sycamore tree to see him: for he was to pass that way. And when Jesus came to the place, he looked up, and saw him, and said unto him, Zacchaeus, make haste, and come down; for today I must abide at thy house. And he made haste, and came down, and received him joyfully. And when they saw it, they all murmured, saying, That he was gone to be guest with a man that is a sinner. And Zacchaeus stood, and said unto the Lord; Behold, Lord, the half of my goods I give to the poor; and if I have taken anything from any man by false accusation, I restore him fourfold. And Jesus said unto him, This day is salvation come to this house, forsomuch as he also is a son of Abraham. For the Son of man is come to seek and to save that which was lost. (Luke 19:2–10 KJV)

Make haste, and come down; for today I must abide at thy house. (Luke 19:5 KJV)

This day is salvation come to this house. (Luke 19:9 KJV)

For the son of man is come to seek and save that which is lost. (Matthew 18:11 KJV)

You may be thinking that your sins are too vile and too many to be forgiven and cleansed. You may be saying, "You don't know the things that I have done. I have done so many evil, sinful, and wicked things in my life. I cannot imagine God being willing to forgive a wretch like me!"

What does the scripture say?

> Where sin abounded, grace did much more
> abound. (Romans 5:20 KJV)

What does that statement mean? God's love for you is so exceedingly abundant that the multitude and vileness of your sins cannot prevent Him from loving you, desiring to forgive you, and saving you from eternal damnation.

The power of the shed blood of Jesus Christ, through His propitiatory sacrifice, is so exceedingly great that it is able to absolve and cleanse the sins—past, present, and future—of the vilest of sinners.

You can see the love of God for forgiving vile sinners who repent by reading about the life of Manasseh, king of Israel in (2 Kings 21:1–17 and 2 Chronicles 33:1–18, paying particular attention to verse 13).

So, my friends and beloved in Christ Jesus, I conclude with the words of the Lord and Savior Jesus Christ Himself:

> For God so loved the world, that he gave his
> only begotten Son, that whosoever believeth in
> him should not perish, but have everlasting life.
> (John 3:16 KJV)

> Greater love hath no man than this, that a
> man lay down his life for his friends. Ye are my
> friends, if ye do whatsoever I command you.
> (John 15:13–14 KJV)

APPENDIX A

AN INTERPRETATION OF JETHRO'S INTEGRITY TEST: OVERALL SCORE

Scores 81–95: Very Good to Excellent Governance

- Their management of the affairs of the state and state resources exceeds or greatly exceeds public expectations.
- Very few areas lack accountability due to very good management of program risks.
- There are very few or negligible public concerns.

Scores 71–80: Good Governance

- Their management of the affairs of the state and state resources meets or exceeds public expectations.
- There are tolerable levels of losses to state resources due to good management of project or program risks.
- There are some public concerns about areas that lack accountability.

Scores 61–70: Unsatisfactory Governance

- Their management of the affairs of the state and state resources somewhat meets public expectations.
- There are intolerable levels of wastage of state resources due to intolerably high levels of incompetence and/or corruption.

- There are public complaints about wastage of state resources.
- There are increasing calls for improvement in the management of the affairs of the state and state resources.
- There are public expressions that the government should be changed, or in the case of a public officer, they should be removed if there is no improvement in the management of the affairs of the state or state resources.

Scores 51–60: Poor Governance

- The public is very dissatisfied with the government's or the public officer's management of the affairs of the state and state resources.
- Their management of the affairs of the state and state resources does not meet public expectations,
- There are highly unacceptable levels of wastage of state resources due to very high levels of incompetence and/ or corruption.
- There is a loud public outcry accompanied by demonstrations and protests.
- There are widespread public calls for a change in government or removal of public officers.

Scores 41–50: Objectionable Governance

- The public is very, very dissatisfied with the government's or the public officer's management of the affairs of the state and state resources.
- The management of the affairs of the state and state resources does not meet public expectations.

- There are objectionable levels of wastage of state resources due to rampant levels of incompetence and/or corruption.
- Vehement public outcries are accompanied by mass demonstrations and protests
- There are vehement widespread public calls for a change in government or the removal of public officers.

Scores 0–40: Atrocious Governance

- The public is extremely dissatisfied with the government's or the public officer's management of the affairs of the state and state resources.
- There are highly objectionable levels of wastage of state resources due to exceedingly rampant corruption and/or gross incompetence.
- Vehement public outcries are accompanied by mass demonstrations and possibly violent protests.
- There are vehement public calls for a change in government or the removal of public officers.

APPENDIX B

BLANK FORM FOR ASSESSING A SINGLE CANDIDATE

Rate Your Representative

Jethro's Integrity Test				
Candidates Name:				
Jethro's Criteria	Weight	Score		Weighted Score
Capable	4			
Fears God	5			
Hates Covetousness	5			
Person of Truth	5			
Overall Score				

APPENDIX C

TIPS FOR IDENTIFYING THOSE FIT FOR PUBLIC OFFICE

They that forsake the law praise the wicked: but such as keep the law contend with them.
> —Proverbs 28:4 KJV

A wicked man accepts a bribe behind the back to pervert the ways of justice.
> —Proverbs 17:23 NKJV

- They refuse bribes and inducements to break the law or circumvent ethical codes of conduct.
- They gesture with their hands and refuse bribes (Isaiah 33:15 NKJV).
- They speak out passionately about wrongdoings in public service and in government.
- They readily advocate and adhere to rules and codes of ethical and professional conduct.
- They are not members of secret societies.

Those who hate covetousness will not:

- accept the invitation to be part of any corporate or government team known to be infested with white-collar criminals.

- have repeated allegations of financial improprieties or scandals over their heads
- have repeated allegations of amassing money, land, houses, and luxury vehicles that their professional income cannot afford
- associate with individuals and organizations known to be involved in questionable financial dealings since birds of a feather flock together
- be repeatedly alleged to have extorted money and property from the ignorant and less fortunate
- subscribe to the view that "politics has its own morality"[24]
- waste state resources via corrupt procurement practices
- help their friends steal their employer's or state resources to obtain financial favors and kickbacks

APPENDIX D

THE PRACTICES OF TYRANTS, DESPOTS, AND FASCISTS

A ruler who lacks understanding is a great oppressor, but he who hates covetousness will prolong his days.

—Proverbs 28:16 (NKJV)

Oppressor is synonymous with despot, tyrant, dictator, overlord, and persecutor.

These are the kind of rulers who will:

- pay to have their opponents or those who know about their evil deeds assassinated
- pervert the course of justice to enable them and their financiers to escape the law and justice
- reach into the offices of independent institutions of state and coerce officers of these institutions to pervert the course of justice under the pretext of acting within the law
- praise those who forsake the laws of God
- establish secrete organizations to spy on their opponents and all who they suspect will expose their evil deeds
- bless the greedy

- establish "mongoose gangs" or secret police to harass those who speak out against their evil deeds
- protect those who are involved in contraband
- be involved in contraband
- protect criminals and money launderers
- institutionalize bribery
- relax or repeal laws that deter contraband
- use their influence to weaken and undermine state security apparatus and institutions to allow their friends, supporters, and financiers who trade in contraband to go undetected
- seek to control the media and feed the population misinformation
- seek to publicly discredit and shame those who are willing to testify about their misdeeds
- mastermind the assassinations of those who are likely to expose their evil deeds
- surround themselves with corrupt individuals
- murder state witnesses
- remove persons of integrity from their inner circles
- manipulate the execution of public policy and procurement practices to enrich themselves and their corrupt friends and families
- embezzle state funds or rape the public purse
- readily break the law, circumvent established norms, practices, and processes, and violate ethical codes of professional conduct in their frenzied scramble to embezzle the state's wealth
- corrupt and interfere with the workings of judicial institutions

APPENDIX E

BLANK FORM FOR EVALUATING A TEAM OF NINE CANDIDATES

Rate Your Team of Candidates

Jethro's Integrity Test: Governance Evaluation												
		Individual Team Members (TM) Scores										
Jethro's Criteria	Weight	TM 1	TM 2	TM 3	TM 4	TM 5	TM 6	TM 7	TM 8	TM 9	Average Score	Weighted Score
Capable	4											
Fears God	5											
Hates Covetousness	5											
Person of Truth	5											
Overall Score												

Instead of using a Microsoft Word Table, Jethro's Integrity Test Table for Teams can be created in Microsoft Excel so that more team members can be added and calculations can be made automatically.

ABOUT THE AUTHOR

Lennox John Grant was born in Trinidad and Tobago and has been a disciple of the Lord Jesus Christ for the past forty-five years. He was married to Shaffina Grant for forty-five years. She has gone home to be with the Lord. Lennox was called to the ministry in 2010 and now pastors the Church of the Gospel of God's Grace, a small assembly of believers at Diego Martin in Trinidad.

ENDNOTES

1   https://www.usatoday.com/story/news/world/2013/06/22/brazil-thousands-protest-anew-but-crowds-smaller/2449229/

2   https://globalvoices.org/2014/08/02/alleged-corruption-in-a-programme-for-disadvantaged-kids-kills-trinidad-tobago-sports-ministers-political-aspirations/

3   https://www.ibtimes.com/kenya-corruption-probe-government-ministers-step-down-president-uhuru-kenyattas-1862594

4   https://www.npr.org/sections/thetwo-way/2015/08/29/435850018/protests-in-malaysia-target-prime-minister-over-alleged-corruption

5   https://www.telegraph.co.uk/news/worldnews/centralamerica andthecaribbean/guatemala/11672415/Thousands-gather-to-protest-government-corruption-in-Guatemala.html

6   https://www.theguardian.com/world/2015/aug/14/honduras-guatemala-protests-government-corruption

7   https://www.politico.com/magazine/story/2015/05/how-new-york-became-most-corrupt-state-in-america-117652

8   https://www.theguardian.com/world/2015/aug/19/canadian-government-faces-widening-corruption-scandal-as-election-looms

9   https://www.forbes.com/2007/04/03/corruption-countries-nations-biz-07caphosp-cx_da_0403corrupt.html#4e709d123fe8

10 https://www.europarl.europa.eu/charter/pdf/text_en.pdf

11 https://rgd.legalaffairs.gov.tt/laws2/Constitution.pdf

12 https://www.biblestudytools.com/lexicons/hebrew/nas/chayil.html

13 https://www.biblestudytools.com/lexicons/hebrew/nas/chayil.html

14 https://rgd.legalaffairs.gov.tt/laws2/Constitution.pdf

15 https://rgd.legalaffairs.gov.tt/laws2/Constitution.pdf

16 https://www.academia.edu/10229929/Nilus_-_The_Great_Within_The_Small

17 https://newsday.co.tt/2017/12/02/politics-own-morality/

18 Webster, Noah. *History of the United States* (307).

---

19 http://libertytree.ca/quotes/Edmund.Burke.Quote.84F1
20 https://www.biblestudytools.com/lexicons/hebrew/nas/checed.html
21 https://www.biblestudytools.com/lexicons/hebrew/nas/checed.html
22 https://legal-dictionary.thefreedictionary.com/diplomatic+immunity
23 https://legal-dictionary.thefreedictionary.com/sovereign+immunity
24 https://books.google.tt/books?redir_esc=y&id=I4wcBgAAQBAJ&q=morality#v=snippet&q=morality&f=false

Printed in the United States
By Bookmasters